Nostalgic
Huddersfield

The publishers would like to thank the following companies for their support in the production of this book

Main Sponsor

Tom Moorhouse & Son Limited

DMD - Roots

Huddersfield New College

Huddersfield Technical College

WT Johnson & Sons (Huddersfield) Limited

ST Shaw Limited

Fred Sheard & Sons

Sam Weller & Sons Limited

First published in Great Britain by True North Books Limited
England HX5 9AE
Telephone: 01422 377977
Copyright © True North Books Limited, 2000

ISBN 1 903204 19 4

Text, design and origination by True North Books Limited
Printed and bound by The Amadeus Press Limited

Introduction

Huddersfield and its surrounding villages nestle into the hills as though they had always been there, and indeed the area has been populated for a very long time, although most of the town centre dates from no earlier than the 19th century.

Archaeological evidence suggests that the first people who had the good sense to make this area their home were the prehistoric Mesolithic tribes, who in 6,000 BC made their homes on the hilltops, since the valleys were too marshy to live in. Their flints and other implements have been found at a number of sites including March Hill.

Much later, between 1500 and 500 BC, the Bronze Age settlers began to trade, making tracks southwards across the hills. They lived in a scattering of small, enclosed settlements, inside which they kept their animals. As time passed, a network of tracks grew up to link the settlements, and throughout the Iron Age trade continued to develop, and the settlements were linked by better tracks. A legacy of this period is the Iron Age hill fort which was discovered at Almondbury, which has left us some useful clues about the inhabitants of the area of that time. They were called Brigantes; their queen was called Cartimandua, and her chief claim to fame was that she betrayed Caractacus when he fled to her after the Roman invasion of Wales (it has to be remembered that these were not true Yorkshire people). Coins have been found bearing the name of Cartimandua and other tribal chieftains such as Volisios and Dunmocoveros.

In spite of Cartimandua's slimy attempts to keep on the right side of the Romans when they arrived in Yorkshire, 28 years after landing in Kent, in 71 AD Petilius Cerialis led an invasion against the Brigantes tribes. He had military bases at Lincoln and Chester, and he must have set up marching camps along the route; it is believed that the earthworks at Meltham are one such memento of his journey.

Even if the Brigantes had not developed the Yorkshire attribute of loyalty, they clearly had some grit, because it seems that at one stage Gnaieus Julius Agricola had to come to the assistance of Petilius Cerialis. The Romans established themselves, and began to grow wheat, grind corn and make bread in stone ovens. They set up an ironworks and a tilery, and may also have made cloth. They departed in 410 AD, leaving the area peaceful and comparatively wealthy. However, subsequent ravages by Saxon pirates, Picts and Scots turned it back into a wasteland.

The Huddersfield we know began to take shape when the Anglian farmers from southern Denmark arrived around 625 AD. Among them was Huder, hence Huder's (or Oder's) field, and Ecgheard, hence Ecgheard's farm (Edgerton). However, their settlement was really centred around Dewsbury. Later, in 950 AD, a contingent of Norsemen took over the higher ground - for instance Fegh (or Fiacc) made his home at Fixby - leaving the Angles on the lower farms. After the 1066 Norman conquest, the district became the property of Ilbert de Lacy. The Domesday Survey tells us that Almannebire (Almondbury) was a relatively large and important place, and Odersfelt was just a small riverside agricultural settlement. In fact Wakefield came to be regarded as the capital of these parts.

There were to be no more territory wars, although in the mid-14th century there sprang up the Eland Feud, a saga of revenge which went on for generations and resulted in the elimination of entire families. By the end of that century Huddersfield was the centre of a growing woollen industry; the many soft water streams in the area were excellent for scouring the wool, and the hillsides were full of sheep, so weavers began coming from other areas to settle in the valley. The men were farmers, and their families used to spin and weave cloth, which was sold at market. Fulling and dyeing was also carried out. The weaver's windows became widespread around this time; designed to let

in as much light as possible, they are an attractive feature of many old properties in the area. Riverside mills were built to finish the cloth, the town grew, and throughout the 16th and 17th centuries trade along the packhorse routes continued to develop. Huddersfield passed into the hands of the Ramsden family, and in 1671 John Ramsden obtained a market charter from Charles ll; at the same time the market in Almondbury ceased, so clearly there had been a switch in the relative importance of the two settlements.

By 1760 the Industrial Revolution had arrived. The woollen industry moved from cottages into big mills, and the machinery such as Kay's 'flying shuttle' was introduced. Meanwhile the town was developing. The canals were opened, and, later, turnpike roads were built. The oval Cloth Hall was built by John Ramsden in 1766, on the site which much later became the ABC cinema. Lockwood brewery was founded in 1795. In 1812 two brothers, Enoch and James Taylor, made a cropping machine, and this marked the beginning of a very colourful period in Huddersfield's history - the Luddite riots. The Colne Valley Museum, in Golcar, has some interesting exhibits from the days when the Luddites went round with a blacksmith's hammer (known colloquially as Enoch's hammer) smashing up the cropping frames, chanting "Enoch (Taylor) has made 'em, and Enoch (the hammer) will break 'em".

Other 19th century developments included the campaign against child labour, in which Richard Oastler, the Factory King, played an important part; the coming (after a certain amount of wrangling) of the railway; the opening of Read Holliday's dyeworks; the growth of Huddersfield's reputation for manufacturing fine worsteds and fancy tweeds; and the development of the engineering industry and quarrying. By 1900, Huddersfield had 100,000 inhabitants and the infra-structure for the town we know today was in place, with gas, electricity and even a public transport system - along with many of the buildings which can be seen in the pages of this book.

Contents

Street scenes

An interesting feature of the tramcar which we see here travelling Route 4, from Marsden to Bradley, is the Post Office letter box affixed to the front of the vehicle. For a small charge, people who had a letter to post could wait at the tram stop and post their stamped letter in the next tram. The boxes used to be emptied twice daily; the last collection during the week was around nine o'clock at night, and five o'clock on a Sunday. So any readers who think that 'value-added service' is a concept thought up by modern businesses, had better think again.... This view dates from the early to mid-1930s. Some of the New Street shop names stayed with us throughout the 20th century - although it seems strange to see Dunn & Co describing themselves as hat-makers, rather than tailors. The distinctive

Marks & Spencer frontage was less than a decade old at the time of this photograph. At the turn of the 20th century, Barrett & Barrett's hardware store stood on the corner of New Street and King Street, with Thornton's Temperance Hotel next door but one. By the 1920s Barrett & Barrett was occupying all three properties. Marks & Spencer then acquired the site which used to be the temperance hotel, and built the frontage seen here. Shortly afterwards, Burton's took over the corner spot from Barrett & Barrett, and constructed their own new frontage which replicated that of the adjoining Marks & Spencer store. The Burton chain also occupied another prime site, on the corner of Market Place and John William Street, so the Burton logo, with its curly lettering, was a very familar sight around town.

There are many interesting details to be picked out on this view of Market Place and John William Street towards the end of the 1930s. In the foreground is one of the old police boxes; some of these were red and some were blue, and we believe this to have been a blue one. The kerb around Rushworth's corner appears to be picked out with black and white stripes, and we assume this was done as a wartime precaution, so that people travelling round town during the blackouts would be able to see where the kerb was. Other potential obstacles to road users, such as lamp posts and vehicle mudguards, were painted white. Rushworth's is just one of the big stores which used to play an important role in Huddersfield

life; when it was first established in the early years of the 20th century, the shop was called the Bazaar. Another favourite old Huddersfield store was Heywoods, which was destroyed by fire. The Great Universal Stores, between Burton's and the YMCA on this picture, also disappeared from the town. Kaye's family-owned business fell victim to the recession in the early 1980s, and around the end of the 20th century many of us were deeply shocked when the Co-op department store closed down. Burton's adopted a more modern image and stayed with us, though not on this spot. Next to Burton's on this photograph is the Refuge Assurance building, which for a long time was the Waverley Temperance Hotel.

Above: Trams and trolley buses were both familiar sights in Huddersfield on 1st April 1939 when this snapshot was taken, though the days of the tram were numbered, and within fifteen months they would have been phased out altogether. In the background is the George Hotel, with its fine stonework looking distinctly black - by the end of the 20th century we were all very concerned about traffic pollution, whereas in the late 1930s it was our coal fires which were responsible for much of the grime and dirt which lingered in the atmosphere. Two of Huddersfield's great claims to fame are represented on this photograph. Firstly, Huddersfield has the distinction of having introduced the first municipal transport service in Britain. Huddersfield Corporation trams started running in January 1883, with the original steam-driven trams replaced by electric in 1901. Secondly, the George Hotel earned a place in the history books in 1895 when Rugby League was born there; inside the hotel is a plaque commemorating the inaugural meeting. Prior to the establishment of the Rugby League there had been no professional rugby players; the Rugby Union was opposed to payment for players and was determined that the sport should remain amateur. The purpose of the new Rugby League was to operate as a professional organisation whose members would be paid.

Above right: New Street was bustling with shoppers when this snapshot was taken in the late 1940s. F W Woolworth's New Street frontage was reduced to virtually nothing in later years, merely retaining access from New Street to allow shoppers to go downstairs into the store. Previously the store had been on two levels, with an upper sales floor at New Street level and a lower sales floor which came out at street level in Victoria Lane, at the rear. Woollies first came to Britain in the early decades of the 20th century with the tag of '3d and 6d Stores', a translation of the American '5 and 10 cent Stores'. The chain was started in America by brothers F W and C S Woolworth in 1879; by 1911 they had over a thousand stores in the USA, and began to establish the chain in other countries. Throughout Britain, Woolworth's became an institution. How many readers began their working lives as Saturday girls at Woollies, we wonder - perhaps on the sweets counter, weighing out quarters of humbugs, chocolate limes, sherbert lemons or jelly babies. Further down New Street is Collinson's Cafe, and in between Collinson's and Woollies at the time of this photograph, concealed by the trolley bus, was a branch of the Fifty Shilling Tailors, at number 45 New Street. The trolley bus is on route 10, for Lockwood. Trolley buses were introduced on this route in February 1939, and some three years later the vehicles were re-numbered, with the new series of numbers beginning at 401.

Nostalgic **HUDDERSFIELD**

From this spot, the Kingsgate Centre, which was under construction at the turn of the 21st century, would probably be just out of sight. We calculate that photographer Morris Bray must have had his back to the old Halifax Building in Cloth Hall Street when he took this snapshot in the 1950s. Subsequently, in July 1979, the Halifax closed its Cloth Hall Street branch; the old building was demolished, and the new concrete and glass building was constructed on the same site and was open for business by September 1981. Such is life - one building comes down and another takes its place. Next door, the Midland Bank had done the same thing around a decade earlier, knocking down its copper-domed 1881 premises, one-time home of the Huddersfield Banking Company, and replacing them with a new building designed by Peter Womersley. A similar fate befell the old Market Hall, down the road in King Street, at roughly the same time. The Market Hall's fine clock tower is plainly visible on this photograph, to bring many a nostalgic memory flooding back. There was tremendous opposition to the plan to demolish the Market Hall; of all the changes which took place in Huddersfield town centre during the 1960s and 70s, this was probably the one which aroused the most feeling. But the old Market Hall closed on 28th March 1970, and the new one opened for business at the beginning of April. Demolition of the old hall started almost immediately, and tragedy struck when the tower collapsed as it was being dismantled, killing two people.

Left: With no trolley bus to be seen, the network of overhead cables appears cumbersome, unnecessary and unsightly to modern eyes. This snapshot of John William Street is believed to date from the early 1950s. Rushworth's, opposite Burton's, would not yet have the clock which later became a landmark. The clock, which worked by electricity, was put up in October 1960, and its twin three-foot dials were visible from Westgate, Kirkgate and John William Street. Henry's, next to Burton's, was one of a number of town centre stores which suffered a dramatic fire during the course of the 20th century; the store was badly damaged when a fire started in its Fairy Grotto in 1947. Booth's clothing factory, towards the back of this view, was the scene of a very bad fire in 1941, and a memorial to those who died was erected in Edgerton Cemetery. Wood's music shop in New Street was set ablaze in January 1964, when a paraffin heater was accidentally knocked over. Heywood's and the Essoldo cinema both suffered fires within a few months of each other towards the end of 1967. The Essoldo was repaired and re-opened, but Heywood's, on the corner of Market Street and Threadneedle Street, was completely destroyed. The popular department store was sadly missed. Confusion seems to have arisen over the subsequent redevelopment of the site, as a supermarket was planned and built but never opened, and in the early 1970s it was redeveloped again for a mixture of retail and office use.

Below: This is a late 1940s view taken from outside the railway station. Trolley buses can be seen loading passengers in John William Street, while one of the Corporation's Joint Omnibus Committee motor buses is heading down Northumberland Street. Huddersfield Joint Omnibus Committee was formed in 1930 as an equal partnership between Huddersfield Corporation and the London, Midland and Scottish Railway Company Limited. To the left of the picture stands the statue of Sir Robert Peel. The Sicilian marble used for this statue was unfortunately not able to withstand the polluted atmosphere of Huddersfield town centre; it began to erode, and by 1949 the statue had deteriorated so badly that it had to be removed. The base went to Ravensknowle Park, and the figure was stored at the Corporation depot in Flint Street, where it quietly disintegrated. It was rumoured at the time that the real reason the statue was taken down was because it showed disrespect to Huddersfield's royal visitors, Princess Elizabeth and the Prince of Wales, when they arrived by train in 1949 - poor Sir Robert had his back turned towards the royal pair when they emerged from the station. More recently, a statue of Huddersfield's famous son Sir Harold Wilson was erected outside the station. He, too, has his back to the station entrance.

Right:
Whatever John Hawkins has put in his shop window, it seems to be attracting a good deal of attention from the ladies! Hawkins' drapery store mostly sold items such as pinafores, overalls, sheets, tablecloths and other household linens. The company had its own works at Green Bank Mill, Preston, where goods were manufactured for sale in the shop. To the right of John Hawkins, on the corner of Cloth Hall Street, is the Fifty Shilling Tailor, or FST for short. This national chain of men's and women's outfitters was established in Huddersfield by the early 1920s, and went on to open a number of branches in the town. By the early 1960s the branch seen here had become John Collier's; the name Fifty Shilling Tailors could hardly be expected to survive in an era when not only could you no longer buy a suit for fifty bob, but shillings themselves were on the way out. Later on, Burton's took the site; Burton's, too, has occupied a series of premises in Huddersfield over the years. At the time of our picture another firm of gentleman's outfitters, Hepworths - who later acquired the services of the Queen's own designer - had the shop the other side of Hawkins. Many more tailors' names will spring to mind: Alexandres, Weaver to Wearer, March - who had the TV jingle 'March the tailors dress you well', while John Collier was 'the window to watch'. Then as now, Huddersfield's menfolk had plenty of choice when it came to outfitters - though most men tended to stay loyal to one shop which they found best suited to their pocket and their taste.

Below: This view of Westgate in the early 1950s shows the road almost devoid of traffic, while in the middle distance a trolley bus is loading for Waterloo. Of an evening, this part of town - top o' t' town, as it was called - was a meeting place for young people. Many a courtship started off with a rendez-vous at Manor's Corner or Cherry Tree Corner or Rushworth's Corner or, and, especially on Saturday nights, from seven o'clock onwards a cluster of boys and girls would be waiting there for their dates. As the clock ticked on, those who were left standing there had to make an agonising decision on just how long they were prepared to wait before considering themselves 'stood up.' In those days, not only did youngsters not have mobile phones, but relatively few families had telephones installed in the house, so keeping in touch was not that simple. If something happened to prevent you from turning up as arranged, there was often no way of letting anybody know. This is another aspect of everyday life which changed drastically during the second half of the 20th century. By the end of the century, most of us had grown accustomed to being able to communicate across the miles virtually at will, and the younger generation in particular would be lost without their mobiles and their e-mail. Three or four decades earlier, we accepted that we could not keep tabs on friends and family 24 hours a day, and arrangements had to be more flexible. In an emergency, or to send special greetings or exciting news, we sent telegrams.

with massive retail parks springing up on the outskirts of towns and enjoying tremendous popularity. How many Huddersfield people at the end of the 20th century had never been to Meadowhall? Surveys showed that shopping had become the nation's number one pastime; but there are still those of us who prefer going to our friendly little corner shops, where you can catch up with the local gossip at the same time. Sadly, the prevalence of retail parks turned these into something of an endangered species.

Top: From this angle, set back from the road behind neat, well-kept flower beds, complete with flag-pole, this large, classically-proportioned Italianate building, with its imposing entrance and ornate masonry, including the great sculpture of Britannia after whom the building is named, looks every bit grand enough to be a town hall. Failing that, it must be a financial institution, since traditionally, the finest buildings in any town or city centre always seemed to belong to banks and building societies. The latter assumption is correct. This solid and stylish piece of architecture was almost exactly a hundred years old when this photograph was taken in August 1956, and had for many decades been the headquarters of the Huddersfield Building Society, established in 1864. No doubt some readers will have arranged the purchase of their first home inside Britannia Buildings. In the early 1950s, when Britain's economy was shaking back down to normal after the second world war, the Huddersfield Building Society was advertising rates of interest of two and a half per cent on shares and two per cent on deposit accounts. That may seem low by 21st century standards, but these things are relative, and inflation was practically non-existent at the time.

Above: The superb Jaguar is heading out of Huddersfield on the Penistone Road, through Fenay Bridge. To the left of the picture is the Star, a very old coaching inn, and off to the right is the turn-off to Almondbury. Since this snapshot was taken, some significant changes in land use have come about in the vicinity of this stretch of road. Further out towards Kirkburton, Storthes Hall, once a mental hospital, became part of the campus of the University of Huddersfield (Huddersfield Polytechnic at the time of the photograph) towards the end of the 20th century, reflecting the growing importance of that institution. A mile or two nearer to town, a major supermarket was built. Supermarkets and self-service shops began to appear after the end of the second world war, marking the end for many small corner shops, which were unable to compete on price and choice. Later still came the trend for out-of-town supermarkets such as the one on Penistone Road, which were undeniably very convenient for motorists. This developed into a whole new phenomenon,

Above: This imposing building once stood on the corner of New Street and Princess Street. The lettering tells us it belonged to the Huddersfield & Upper Agbrigg Savings Bank, established in 1918. The very name of the institution harks back to a time when most communities of sufficient size had their own bank and building society, which local people would automatically use and look upon as 'their' bank. Unmistakably Yorkshire institutions included the Barnsley Permanent Building Society, the Bradford and Bingley Building Society, the Skipton Building Society, the Halifax and Huddersfield Union Bank, which later merged with the Halifax Joint Stock Bank to form the West Yorkshire Bank, and the Yorkshire Penny Bank. This latter concern was founded in 1856 by Colonel Edward Akroyd of Halifax, under the impressive title of The West Riding of Yorkshire Provident Society and Penny Savings Bank. Over the years, banking institutions spread and amalgamated, and by the end of the 20th century relatively few retained any real connection with the place where they had originated. Even the Yorkshire Bank's connection with Yorkshire was in name only, the business itself having been taken over by an overseas institution. Already when this photograph was taken in 1964, the Huddersfield & Upper Agbrigg Savings Bank was displaying a newer sign bearing the more anonymous title of Trustee Saving Bank. As the century progressed, banking became increasingly automated and faceless, with holes-in-the-wall, telephone banking and Internet banking, and the old days when people knew their bank manager personally, and overdrafts and other transactions were arranged in wood-panelled offices that smelt of pipe-smoke, were gone.

Despite the overhead trolley wires and the presence of two-way through traffic along New Street, this 1956 view is made instantly recognisable by the Prudential Buildings on the right. This distinctive and ornate brick edifice graced the corner of Ramsden Street and New Street throughout virtually the whole of the 20th century, having been erected in 1901 at a cost of £9,260. It was designed by the famous Victorian architect Alfred Waterhouse. Originally the whole building served as offices for the Prudential Assurance Company, but the ground floor was converted to shops in 1938, and remained that way. Conversely, throughout the first part of the 20th century the Commercial Hotel's corner was shared by a

tobacconist's, as seen here, but this later disappeared and the entire premises became the Commercial Hotel. Adjoining it, off the photograph to the left, is the fanciest building in High Street, with many ornate features including faces carved above the Gothic-style window arches, and an archway with impressive iron gates leading into a courtyard. Sadly this fantastic architectural specimen ended the 20th century empty and forlorn. The roofline down the left hand side of New Street changed significantly in the early 1970s when the old Midland Bank building, whose distinctive copper dome can be seen on this photograph, was replaced by the tall square structure which now juts up against the skyline at the corner of Cloth Hall Street.

All those headscarves might lead readers to make a shrewd guess at the date of this photograph. It was in fact taken in December 1958. Queen Elizabeth herself set the fashion for headscarves, and once we discovered their practical advantages - they kept the ears warm, they did not blow off in the wind, and you could stuff them inside a coat pocket or up a sleeve when you took your coat off so you didn't have to worry about losing them - many of us were reluctant to give them up, even when the trend-setters told us firmly that they had become, as it were, old hat. The group is being seen safely across the road by a policeman; by 1958, Huddersfield was well used to using zebra crossings. The first pedestrian crossings were one of Transport Minister Leslie Hore-Belisha's great contributions to road safety. Launched in 1934, crossings were originally marked out by studs and dotted lines on the road, and beacons with black and white striped posts and glass bowls, which gave out an orange glow. The glass bowls made a wonderful target for little boys with stones, so they had to be replaced by yellow painted aluminium globes until unbreakable plastic bowls were developed in 1952. Then all that remained was to educate people into using pedestrian crossings. Various schemes have been tried out over the years to teach children the principles of road safety - did you join the Tufty Club when you were at school?

Below: On 9th March 1960, Leeds City Transport's tramcar number 526 was saying its farewells to Yorkshire. Its destination was the USA, where preservation and hopefully a long and secure future awaited it. The tramcar was transported to the docks by road, by Pickfords Ltd, and the route involved passing under Thornton Lodge railway bridge. As we can see from this photograph, delicate manoeuvring is called for to avoid getting tangled up with the trolley bus overhead wiring which runs underneath the bridge. Workmen from Huddersfield Corporation have been called out to guide the high load safely through, and a tower wagon is standing by in case of mishap. During the tram and trolley bus eras, towers such as this one were used to repair the overhead power network when wear and tear took its toll. Since they were used when power failed, they obviously had to be motorised, although there also used to be a number of horse-drawn tower wagons in the tramway days. The vehicle seen in this photograph is a post-war AEC.

Bottom: The location of this bustling scene, captured by the camera on a sunny day in the 1960s, will be familiar to any reader who lived in Huddersfield at that time. Sadly the fine stone building that was Huddersfield's old Market Hall, in King Street, found no place in the town centre redevelopment plans, and within a decade of this photograph it was gone - but not forgotten. Upstairs was a bookshop, Berry's the drapers, and a cafe which did a good pie and peas. There was Redman's, which moved to the new market; there was a hardware store, there were sweet stalls which sold loose

sweets, and there was d'Agostino's ice cream. And there was Dr Dan's drink stall; Dr Dan sold a very special patent herbal drink with secret ingredients, which would set you back a penny or tuppence, depending on whether you needed a large or a small glass. Outside the Market Hall there were stalls down Shambles Lane, and a Dolls' Hospital along the top side. In fact, looking back, it seems there was everything for everyone - a choice of greengrocers so that careful shoppers could make housekeeping stretch further, a newsagent where kiddies could spend their pocket money on comics.... Most people's reaction, on looking at this photograph, is likely to be along the lines of, 'They should never have pulled it down.' The resident rats were no doubt of the same opinion; when the building was demolished, it was reported that a whole army of homeless rats fled for their lives.

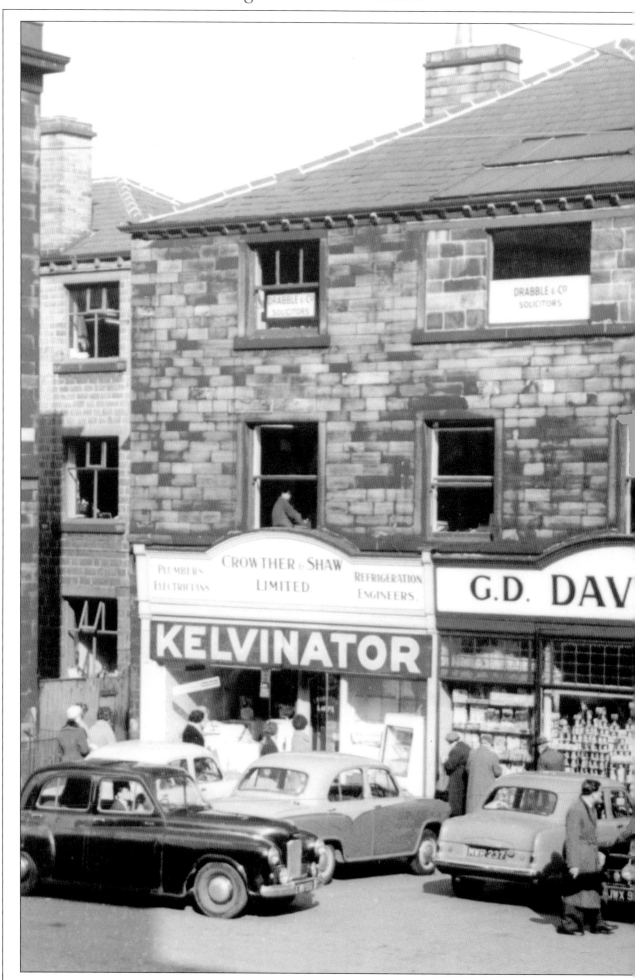

This was the view that used to greet you as you emerged into Market Street from the Ritz Cinema in 1959. Above your heads were the tram cables, opposite was Crowther's, next to that was GD Davies the grocers, and round the corner in Cloth Hall Street was Paints (Huddersfield) Limited. Paints had recently opened a first floor wallpaper showroom which claimed to be the first of its kind in the district. The DIY culture was growing rapidly around this time, largely as a result of new developments in paints, glues and synthetic building materials, which made products more user-friendly and enabled unskilled workmen - or women - to do their own decorating and home improvements with perfectly adequate results, and more cheaply than if they had called in the professionals. In fact, when the major paint manufac-turers came to market these new products, they were very wary of explicitly targeting the amateur decorator, as they feared that by doing so they would alienate their traditional client base of trade customers - and they were not sure whether the public would buy. They need not have worried; Dulux, launched onto the retail market in 1953, soon became a household name, and the trade accepted that a new market had opened up. During the 1950s and 60s we turned into a nation of keen DIY-ers. However, Paints (Huddersfield) had been in on the act for a long time before that. The firm was actually set up in 1924, specifically to retail paint to the home decorator, which makes it a very early forerunner of the DIY movement.

High days & holidays

Nostalgic **HUDDERSFIELD**

As usual, Holmfirth's 1953 Brass Band Festival in Victoria Park has drawn a huge crowd. Brass bands have been part of Yorkshire life since the early 19th century, and it is recorded that the very first Yorkshire brass band contest was held at Burton Constable Hall, near Hull, in 1856. Sheffield staged a similar contest in 1858. As time went on the calendar filled up with band competitions. The annual Holmfirth contest was always a popular one. No Huddersfield Summer Entertainment programme would have been complete without a band contest. National organisations such as the Coal Board and the Co-op ran national competitions for their own bands. Towns and villages organised band competitions. The two really big events were the Belle Vue September Brass Band Championship, now known as the British Open, and the National Championship which was sponsored for many years by the Daily Herald. For the latter, regional heats were held, and competitors were graded into four sections, with a different test piece for each. In the post-war years, bands' repertoires began to grow much more varied, with music being composed especially for brass bands for the first time. Granville Bantock (who was associated with the London Royal Academy of Music) and Thomas Keighley were probably the first two to do this; Bantock's first brass band piece was Prometheus Unbound, and Keighley's was Northern Rhapsody. The trend continued, and as more new works were written which explored the full potential of each brass instrument, afternoons around the bandstand became even more pleasurable for crowds like this one.

Below: Brass bands are an important part of the Yorkshire culture. Traditionally, just about every big firm had its band; villages had their band, sometimes more than one, and, as everybody who has seen the film Brassed Off will know, collieries had their bands. With so many bands around, a certain amount of rivalry was inevitable, and a healthy competitive spirit grew up which helped raise the standard of performance all round - as well as giving the players an opportunity to perform to an appreciative audience. The 1950s brought many competition successes for the Hepworth Silver Prize Band, pictured here in 1952 at Huddersfield Town Hall. This band is reported to have been formed around the early 1870s, and was very successful around the turn of the 20th century. Then, for one reason and another, a number of its members left - some to join the newly-formed Hade Edge Band - and for a period the Hepworth band found itself short of players and struggling. However, after the end of the second world war the band's fortunes took a distinct turn for the better. These bandsmen can look forward to an excellent run of success as the decade draws to a close - including second prize at Belle Vue in 1957, first prize at Belle Vue in 1958, first prize at Bury in 1959, and first prize at Holmfirth in 1960. Under their new conductor, Mr Kaye, the Hepworth Prize Band added some of the more difficult pieces to their repertoire, and earned themselves a reputation as a band of well above-average competence.

Do these youngsters, posing nonchalantly in the playground at Greenhead Park in 1950, know that when the playground was opened a generation or so earlier it was strictly for use by the under-nines? It was originally known as the Richard Oastler Playground. Richard Oastler, dubbed The Factory King, was steward to the Thornhill Estate from 1820 to 1838, and lived at Fixby Hall. His energetic campaigning for the rights of children included fighting for the Ten Hours Bill to restrict the number of hours which children were required to work. He also wrote extensively, and as author of a number of publications including Fleet Papers he became a well-known and respected figure. A number of his letters to the Press, including one published in the Leeds Mercury in 1830 under the title of Yorkshire Slavery, stirred up a good deal of public reaction. At one stage he was also a candidate for Parliament, and he opposed the Poor Law Amendment Act of 1834. There was a great deal of local support for Mr Oastler, and naming the new playground after him, many years after his death, was a nice gesture and a fitting tribute to a man who had devoted so much of his life to paving the way so that future generations of children - like the ones seen on this photograph - would be liberated from a life of drudgery, and able to enjoy what we now consider to be a normal childhood.

Left: Huddersfield is fortunate in having so many parks and open spaces both in the town centre and scattered around the outskirts. During the 1950s, when this photograph was taken, the Town Guide listed, amongst its Open Spaces, Greenhead Park, at thirty-six acres, Beaumont Park at twenty-five and a half acres, Ravensknowle Park at twelve acres, and Norman Park at eight and a half acres; also Leeds Road Playing Fields, and sixty small recreation grounds totalling some three hundred and fifty acres altogether. Townsfolk have enjoyed their most central park, Greenhead, for well over a century. The land used to belong to Benjamin Haigh Allen, and later to the Ramsden family. The town then acquired the site from the Ramsden Estate, at a cost of £1,000 per acre, and the park was opened in September 1884. Greenhead Hall was demolished in 1909 and the Girls' High School - later Greenhead College - was built on its site. In 1924 the Park was extended by almost five acres, and two putting greens, two bowling greens and fourteen tennis courts were constructed on the new piece of land, providing the town with outdoor sports facilities to be proud of. Five years later a Conservatory was built near the main entrance, and in 1934 a paddling pool was constructed for the children, but subsequently filled in. Later in the 20th century car ownership enabled families to travel to out-of-town attractions; but Huddersfield's parks, Greenhead in particular, continue to play an important role in our lives as a place of recreation and relaxation when we don't feel like going far from home.

Above: Greenhead Park used to have a lake with swans on it and a paddling pool, but these water features have long gone. The iron railings which prevented small children from coming to a watery end were sacrificed as part of the war effort, and afterwards the lake and pool were deemed health and safety hazards, and were closed off, drained and filled in. The flat grassy area behind the bandstand now marks the spot were the lake once was. Splashing around in a paddling pool on a sunny day, in a picturesque setting, is an excellent way for children to learn to feel at home in the water, and this used to be a very popular venue for Huddersfield's youngsters. Most readers will remember their swimming lessons at school - what an achievement it was when you could swim down the deep end! Pupils were encouraged to take their 'third class', and some went on to achieve 'second class' or 'first class' swimming certificates. Third class, if memory serves, simply involved swimming for a specified distance without stopping or touching the rail. Of course, swimmers in Huddersfield during the 60s were spurred on by the example of our very own world champion swimmer, Anita Lonsbrough, who won the gold medal for the 200 metre breast stroke at the 1960 Olympic Games in Rome. Swimming events were regularly shown on TV, so we had many an opportunity to sit in our armchairs with our eyes glued to the flickery black and white screen, cheering for Anita Lonsbrough.

No wonder this lot - pictured in the paddling pool at Greenhead Park in June 1950 - were in such high spirits: the sun was out, they had the summer holiday to look forward to, and once again a full Summer Entertainment Programme had been organised. This tradition began in 1941, when the Huddersfield Holidays at Home programme was planned specifically to provide entertainment for those unable to go away on holiday because of the war. It was such a success that after the war a similar scheme, subsequently known as the Summer Entertainments Programme, continued to be organised each summer in Greenhead Park. There were roundabouts, magic shows, pony rides and Punch and Judy; there were concerts and talent-spotting contests; there were miniature railways; there were bowls competitions, draughts matches and tennis tournaments; in fact, there was just about everything you could think of. And it became traditional for the programme to end with a grand firework display. The Entertainments became an important part of Huddersfield life, and the Corporation went to great lengths to maintain the high standard it had set. Many readers will remember the late Mr Frank Crosland, who did invaluable work in organising the Entertainments for many years; his was the voice which boomed out announcements over the loudhailer. Mr Crosland also assisted with Thespian productions, and former Thespians will recall how particular he was about safety on the stage. Lighted candles, for instance, were never seen on-stage in a production arranged by Mr Crosland.

On stage beneath the simple but effective starry backdrop are Max Jessop's Jazz Band, playing at the David Brown Dance in December 1963. Although unfortunately we have no information about Max Jessop, we do know something about Joe Jessop. Well over a century ago, seven-year old Joe Jessop was a cornet player with the Huddersfield Temperance Band. It is also recorded that Joe used to specialise in performing, as it were, a solo duet, in which he played cornet and piano at the same time! For the staff at the big local firms like David Brown's, the Christmas 'do' was always something to look forward to. Some long-established firms still uphold this tradition, but other companies now favour a more modern style of management, and use 'team-building exercises' as a means of fostering team spirit. Staff development and appraisal had risen high on the agenda for management by the end of the 20th century, but in the 1950s a very important aspect of being a good boss was to provide the wherewithal for everybody to eat, drink, dance and be merry at Christmas.

Bill Malbert's father, on the other hand, was a workman on the railway, and Bill himself - so the story goes - was born in a workmen's hut beside the railway tracks. Whether this is true or not, Bill was a true original, and people were never short of a topic of conversation or a smile when he was around.

Top: Here's a scene which will bring back memories for the many readers who have been involved in amateur operatics over the years - and especially for long-standing members of Woodhouse Amateur Operatic Society. Our photograph has captured a colourful moment from their April 1954 production of 'The Desert Song'. Even in Huddersfield, with its

Above: Each generation of Huddersfield folk seems to produce its share of 'characters'. Making 'em all smile in this photograph is Mr Bill Malbert, who became something of a local legend around the middle of the 20th century. A genial figure with his waistcoat, hat and stick, Bill was so well known around the pubs that he rarely had to buy his own pint. He was one of those larger-than-life figures that we somehow expect to live for ever, simply because we know that life just wouldn't be the same without them - rather like the nation's favourite Queen Mum, mother of Queen Elizabeth II. Bill certainly gave it his best shot, reaching, we are reliably informed, the grand old age of 100 - again, like the Queen Mum. But if we are to believe the tales which circulated, the circumstances of Bill Malbert's birth were rather different to those of the Queen Mum's. The future wife of King George VI was born Lady Elizabeth Bowes-Lyon, daughter of the 14th Earl of Strathmore.

strong musical traditions, changing lifestyles during the latter part of the 20th century led to a decline in the number of people joining operatic societies, and sadly many of the smaller groups ceased to exist when they were no longer able to get together a full cast. Among those which survived and continue to entertain us into the third millennium are Longwood Amateurs, Lindley Amateurs, Huddersfield Amateur Operatic, Huddersfield Light Opera - who also do pantomime - and, of course, the stars of this photograph, Woodhouse Amateur Operatic Society. During the latter part of the 20th century Woodhouse was particularly fortunate in recruiting a young and talented cast, enabling them to present more modern and experimental works, with a cabaret flavour. Many societies bemoan the shortage of romantic male leads - so perhaps some of the personable young men amongst our readership would like to volunteer their services!

irk Bogarde, whose name heads the bill for the Ritz's main film 'For Better For Worse' on this photograph from January 1955, had become a major box-office star the previous year as Dr Simon Sparrow in 'Doctor In The House'. 'For Better For Worse' was a rather unmemorable film about newly-weds. Its title is reminiscent of Bogarde's acting debut as the juvenile in 'When We Are Married', at a small suburban theatre in 1939. From there, the Hampstead-born actor took many small parts in rep, and in 1946, after his war service, he appeared in 'Power Without Glory'. This, again, was a small theatre production, but with Kenneth More in the cast it attracted critical acclaim, was transferred to the West End, and was televised, thus opening up new doors for Bogarde. He signed a

contract with the Rank Organisation, and after many minor parts his first big role came about by default. In 1948 he was cast as the priest in 'Esther Waters', with Stewart Granger playing the lead; however, Stewart Granger then decided not to accept the role, and it was given to Bogarde instead. Other Bogarde films included the thriller 'Hunted' in 1952, in which he was particularly well reviewed, but it was 'Doctor

In The House' which made him a household name. And if he got his first major part almost by chance, then fate cheated him out of another role which might have proved the high spot of his career: he was to star in a £1.5 million Rank production of 'Lawrence of Arabia' in the late 1950s - but the entire project was cancelled. Rank never made the film, but a different version was released in 1962.

A moving family story

July 1887 was a great time of celebration in the Moorhouse household, not only was Fred, a son and heir born to Tom and Charlotte, but Tom also took the far-reaching step of going into business on his own.

Tom had been a Teamer, a man who drove the horses for Donkersleys a local firm of dyers and finishers at Lord's Mill on Magdale when he decided to work for himself. The timing was fortunate because Sam Sykes who had been the local carrier around the Honley area of Huddersfield was hoping to retire and Tom bought the business from him for £41 in July 1887, a document recording the transaction is still in the possession of the Moorhouse family today.

Tom and Charlotte lived originally in the Thirstin district of Honley, moving to 2 Marsh, Honley around the turn of the century, where they had a house, stabling for the horses and a barn. Tom ran his business from home and his daily tasks to begin with included carrying

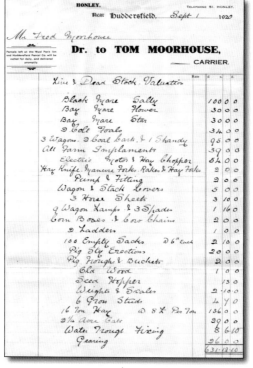

parcels for members of the local community; later he developed contacts with local textile firms and carried regular consignments of woollen cloth up and down the Holme Valley, sometimes even going as far as Manchester in the days when a journey of that distance by horse and wagon took a full day and what a day it was! They would have to set off at midnight and would get back home 24 hours later! He also undertook work for Honley Urban District Council, often clearing snow during the heavy snowfalls usual in the area at the time. For this Tom was paid 30 shillings a week; a reasonable weekly wage at the time was 18 shillings and out of the remaining 12 shillings he had to feed and stable his horse, so there wasn't a great deal of profit in the job.

Local quarries found Tom to be reliable and employed the firm to transport locally hewn stone. The firm was responsible for

Above: Bill of transfer from the founder to his two sons - September 1920. *Below:* Founder with 'Sally' c 1908.

The business thrived in the years leading up to the first world war owing to many local engineering and textile companies entrusting their goods to the firm's care. The war years were busy as Tom Moorhouse & Son was in the enviable position of being the only carrier in the Honley area. Tom and his family had seized the opportunity of acquiring land when it became available and had also gone into farming in a small way, thereby making them involved in 'reserved' occupations and therefore not liable to be called up. The youngest son, however, Herbert did go away to fight and was taken prisoner by the Germans.

carrying the stone used in the construction of Moorbottom Chapel in Honley.

Business prospered and during the course of time Tom took on two more teamers; he owned eight horses and four or five wagons and carts. Tom and Charlotte's family, when complete consisted of four sons and a daughter. Two sons, Arthur and Fred joined their father in the business, another son John Richard worked in a railway wagon builders at Lockwood, Herbert worked in a mill as a tuner and in keeping with the practice of the time, their daughter Emily helped her mother in the home.

Fred, who was working for his father married, in 1914, Sarah Elizabeth Asquith who had been born in Barnsley and worked 'in service' locally.

Perhaps there were family disagreements regarding the future of the company and its response to the massive changes in society brought about by the Great War and

Above left: *Fred Moorhouse with one of his 'charges' c 1903.* ***Top:*** *George V's Silver Jubilee celebration, 1935 with driver Harry Cunningham.*

the developing technology of the motor wagon - Fred wanted to meet the challenges of the new era by expanding into motor transport, his father perhaps found the prospect of an entirely new way of operating too much to cope with - whatever happened, the result was that Tom decided to retire and he sold the firm to his two sons, Arthur and Fred. These two went onto partnership on 1 September, 1920. A 'Live and Dead Stock Evaluation' done at the time puts the value of the company's assets at £631 12s 10d which included £100 for a black mare named Sally, hay knife, manure forks, rakes and hay forks valued at £2, 100 empty sacks at 6d each making a total of £2 10s and 16 tons of hay at £8 per ton, £136 in all.

A company letterhead of the time gives the telephone number as Honley 51 and states 'Parcels left at the Wool Pack Inn and Huddersfield Parcel Co. will be called for daily, and delivered promptly'.

Fred and Arthur soon acquired two left hand drive Model T Fords, each of which enabled them to make deliveries much more quickly. Perhaps out of affection for the horses that had served them so well and so long they were reluctant to dispose of them all and there is a record of them still having one horse at the start of the 1930s.

By now Fred had a family of his own, son Stanley and a daughter, Rachel and was keen to move the business forward. His brother and business partner Arthur, however was not in good health and so Fred offered to buy Arthur out - this happened in 1932 when the partnership was dissolved and Fred, like his father before him, was on his own. He seized the opportunity of being able to expand the business by investing in

Above: *New Albion Chieftain at Honley Show loaded with two David Brown Cropmaster tractors in 1950.*
Top: *Albion Clansman on Honley Carnival duty at Moorbottom, Honley, 1958.*

more vehicles and by accepting work from further afield. He purchased part of the present day premises in 1936 - a garage and workshop from S Drake Corn Millers for £695. An enclosed motor garage was built by Fred and his team who between them had all the necessary skills. To celebrate the completion of the building, Fred's wife made an enormous meat and potato pie for everyone who had been involved with the new building.

It was a time of financial hardship for the Moorhouse family - money needed to be found both to buy Arthur out and buy the original premises from Tom at Marsh, Honley. However, since the general standard of living was not as high as it is today and no doubt the satisfaction and excitement of developing a business in a forward-looking way made up for some of the deprivations they had to cope with at the time.

There were also other events which lightened the mood at the time. In keeping with the firm's strong connection with the locality, Tom Moorhouse & Son provided an open-backed wagon to transport a party of local children in the village procession on the occasion of the coronation of King George VI on 12 May 1937. A profusion of roses form a backdrop for the village 'Queen' and her attendants and the wagon was patriotically decked out with numerous Union Jacks and the lorry side bore the inscription 'God Bless Our King'. Fred had settled on purchasing what he considered to be the most suitable vehicles for the job and rapidly built up a fleet of seven Morris Commercial vehicles. By the beginning of the second world war he was

carrying coal for Honley Co-op, millwrights, engineers and textile firms. An example of a long distance job at the time was a ruling machine transported from John Shaw & Sons to the East end of London for the princely sum of £7 10s. War-time conditions have a habit of playing havoc with the expectations of normal business life and Fred had his own experience of this when a new vehicle he had acquired was commandeered for the war effort and was taken away with the paint still wet.

The average wage for a mill worker at the time was £2 10s a week, however Fred was careful to treat his men more fairly and he paid three guineas a week as well as the National Insurance stamp. He provided clean overalls for his staff and generally looked after them well. This way he ensured he always had the best possible drivers for the wagons.

The early 1940s were a time of great difficulty for Fred who carried on the business without the manpower he really needed. By this time the second world war had loomed and Fred's son Stanley was away in the RAF for four-and-a-half -years.

There were other pressures too - Bob Hanson, father of the famous Lord Hanson was keen to buy Fred out and made a number of offers for the business. Fred had to decide what to do for the best, and at one time was seriously considering accepting.

Below: *Taking part in George VI's celebrations was a Morris Commercial in Church Street, Honley in 1937.*

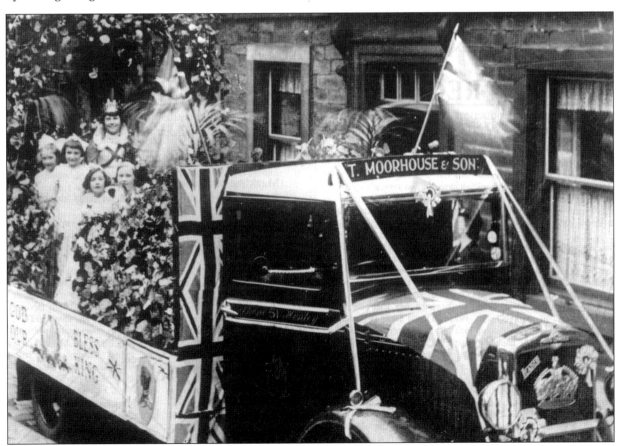

It was his daughter, Rachel who persuaded him to hold on to the family business so that Stanley would have the business to come back to once the war was over.

Stanley had joined the firm at 14 years of age in 1935. Both he and his sister had attended Kayes College, Huddersfield. To begin with Rachel worked only part-time in the business as she had office jobs in two local mills before devoting herself fully to the family concern around 1938.

Having a fleet of vehicles was one thing, keeping them in good running order during the war was quite another. The company had been fortunate in securing the services of Lupton Littlewood who joined the firm in 1935. He had served an apprenticeship at Karrier Motors and was a skilled motor engineer. It was to a large extent his ingenuity in 'make do and mend' repairs that ensured the business was kept on the road.

But better days were ahead. For a start the war did not go on for ever and Stanley, unlike thousands of his contemporaries, came home. The very fact that he had continued to trade through the difficult war years meant that Fred had accumulated enough capital to replace worn out vehicles steadily as new ones became available. He replaced the fleet with vehicles from CH Mitchells, the local Morris agent.

The company was incorporated in 1947 and Stanley became a partner with his father. Tom Moorhouse & Son were undertaking more furniture removals as a result of the housing boom of the late 1940s and increased prosperity generally. Over the years this aspect of the business was to play an increasingly important role. The firm also became involved in delivering David Brown tractors through 'Transports Huddersfield' of East Parade.

Throughout this period there was the threat of the nationalisation of the road haulage industry; Fred, in his capacity of Chairman of the Huddersfield Road Haulage Association, a position he held for 5 years, did all he could to prevent the taking over of his business. In the end he was able to achieve this due to the fact that the majority of the firm's work was concentrated within a 25 mile radius of Honley. The early 1950s unfortunately saw a deep recession in the textile industry.

In an attempt to maintain the volume of work, Fred and Stanley acquired another local removals company, Raymond Senior (Haulage and Storage) Ltd., paying £3,000 for the privilege. The share holding was divided amongst members of the family - Fred had a 50 per cent share, Stanley 25 per cent and Rachel's husband Arthur the remaining 25 per cent. This venture did not fit in with the Moorhouse operation as expected, however, and the new firm was eventually sold on to a local removals firm, F Mawer & Son.

The company continued to prosper through development and change. Rachel's husband Arthur joined the firm as a driver in 1952 and a new garage was built at the Honley depot in 1954. The fleet at this time was changing over from petrol engined Morris Commercials to diesel engined Albions.

Stanley had married Joan Broadbent, the youngest daughter of another haulage family whose business E B Broadbent was based in Penistone, in 1951. They had three children, Timothy, Chris and Josie.

The 1950s was a time of consolidation and growth, the fleet being expanded slightly. Important to the company during this period was the business it secured from Magdale Vinery which involved transporting products like VP Wines, QC Sherry and Babycham. Times were changing - deliveries of coke from Huddersfield gas works to local chapels became a thing of the past, and in 1959 the firm carried out its last removals assignment.

In 1961 the old Co-operative Hall was acquired and adapted for the purpose as an extension of the haulage depot and workshop.

Above: *Stanley with eldest son, Timothy, c 1955.*

During this time the firm's association with the Honley Show was inaugurated. Fred was its President from 1952 till a month before his death in 1963. It played a big part in his life and was of great interest during his last years. The contact continues to this day as the firm still do all moving and transport for the Honley Show Society.

Fred died in June 1963, after giving in excess of 60 years dedication to the company and was carried appropriately from the family homestead at Marsh, Honley to Moorbottom Chapel on one of his own wagons.

Following his father's death, Stanley assumed full control of the company, and continued to operate it according to the principles which had served his father so well, seeking to expand the fleet and scope of the business, and still operating from Honley. His eldest son Timothy left school and went to work for Reliance Garage Company, Brighouse as an apprentice mechanic. Due to family circumstances he left and went to E B Broadbent at Penistone, which was the other haulage business in the family, in November 1969, to learn the ropes of their business. Timothy ended up running the company some years later.

This heralded a time of increased co-operation between the two companies which are, of course related by the marriage of Stanley and Joan. There were numerous opportunities for mutual advantage as the Moorhouse operation was chiefly in four wheel rigid vehicles and Broadbents having articulated vehicles.

In 1970 Chris joined his father in the firm straight from school as a driver's mate and apprentice mechanic and worked over the years as a driver and maintenance supervisor;

Left: *David Brown Trackmaster loaded for London on a Morris Commercial - 1949, driven by Duncan Bradley.*
Top: *A fleet line-up of Morris Commercials in 1939.*

he also acted as Company Secretary and generally helping with the running of the business. Frank Wood, Stanley's right-hand man in the company's office died suddenly after being with the firm 24 years. In that year Brian Gledhill who had been the fleet mechanic with the company also died suddenly and the firm suffered further loss in 1973 on the death of Arthur, Rachel's husband. These were all key people who had made important contributions to the firm and upon whom Stanley had relied for many years and he felt their loss deeply.

Stanley had to take on the lion's share of the office work and Joan and Rachel helped out by diong the weekly wages. Josie Moorhouse left school in 1974. She had also attended Kayes College like her father and came straight to work for the family business, learning the ropes along the way from her father. She had always had a nose for the haulage business, which is not too surprising, and even as a young child knew how to

handle large trucks; she was sitting in one when the handbrake hadn't been properly applied and the truck, scarily, started to move towards the river. Showing great presence of mind she went straight to the handbrake and gave it a mighty pull. Perhaps six pennorth of sweets has never been earned in a more deserving way! In 1974 more office space was purchased at the Honley site and more land and parking space was acquired at the same time.

The company celebrated its centenary in July 1987 and the staff and family celebrated in style. Stanley took the opportunity to hand over the business to

Above: *New Albion Chieftain - September 1961.*
Right: *June 1963 - Albion Claymore taken at Huddersfield Crematorium at the funeral of Fred Moorhouse.*

transport scene to satisfy their customers' various needs and requirements.

Josie and Chris. His retirement was one in name only, however, as he carried on driving and helping out in many other ways right up until February 1994. At the centenary celebrations opportunity was taken to recognise the long service of three of the employees; Duncan Bradley (38 years service), Herbert Beardsell (24 years service) and Ronnie Shaw (also 24 years service). Ronnie Shaw is still with the company today. That year also saw the firm starting to operate curtain sided vehicles to meet customers' ever-changing requirements.

1990 saw the acquisition of the company's first articulated vehicle. It was purchased solely to work for what is now one of Moorhouse's largest customers who are one of the country's foremost producers of laminated chipboard. Since then the company has seen the need for artics increase and now runs a fleet of ten, alongside the rest of its mixed fleet.

Present-day customers include one of the country's leading aluminium anodisers, also one of the country's largest chipboard laminators and a premier producer of hot beverages, as well as moving raw coffee beans from warehouses in Kent to customers throughout the UK. The company also moves large quantities of polypropylene which is produced locally.

Today Chris Moorhouse and his sister Josie Galloway work in tandem running the business; Chris is in charge of the day-to-day running of the firm, along with other key and valued members of staff. He also oversees the maintenance and repairing of the fleet. Josie is in charge of administration and accounts from the company's office in the Lake District, where she lives with her husband and children, making weekly visits to Honley to deal with any matters arising on site. The company is proud to occupy a prominent position in the West Yorkshire road haulage industry, moving with the times and adjusting to developments in the

The firm has weathered the various storms affecting the road haulage industry spanning three centuries and has responded to the challenges made upon them. The energies of four generations of the Moorhouse family have have been spent in adapting to an ever-changing economic climate in industry needs and recent challenges have included conforming to new legislation and coping with ever-increasing running costs. The founder's great grand-children, Timothy, Chris and Josie, have been extremely proud to have been involved in the writing of the company's history and are deeply concious of the traditions of the company which are; quality, civility, service and satisfaction.

Above left: *Chris Moorhouse's 'new pride and joy', a DAF 2100 in September 1980 at Greenhead Park.*
Above right: *Josie Moorhouse with one of the firm's drivers, Duncan Bradley taken at the centenary celebrations in 1987.* ***Below:*** *One of the company's latest 6 axle 41 tonne G.T.W artics in a major customer's livery.*

Action replay

Above: This snapshot was taken at Maine Road, Manchester. Huddersfield Town supporters had crossed the Pennines - along with their mascot - to support their team in the 1928 FA Cup Semi-Final against Sheffield United. The match attracted a record crowd of 69,360, and an Alec Jackson goal thrilled Town supporters, paving the way for their team's first Wembley appearance in the 1928 Cup Final. Town were going strong and looked to be well on course for the century's first 'double', but unfortunately they had an off-day and crashed 1-3 to Blackburn.

Above right: Here we see the Huddersfield Town and Burnley skippers, dressed in the height of 1940s football fashion - rather a different spectacle from the skimpy shorts worn by the long-haired George Best and his generation, a couple of decades later! Peter Doherty, captain of Town, is welcoming ex-Town half-back Alan Brown (in the Number 5 shirt) back to his old stamping-ground. Brown has returned as captain of Burnley, to make his first appearance at Leeds Road since leaving the club. The match, in December 1947, was played to a packed stadium with a crowd of almost 40,000.

Nostalgic **HUDDERSFIELD**

This was an instance of football hooliganism, 1930s style.... In the pre-war days, wherever a big crowd gathered, pickpockets could always be expected to be out in force. Gangs of pickpockets would often attach themselves to the London football clubs which attracted large travelling support. Here, victims whose pockets have been picked have been keen to take the law into their own hands and have attacked a suspect.

Police are restraining the crowd while the man who has been 'done over' is being revived by an ambulanceman. The crowd of spectators is strikingly different from a late 20th century football crowd - no football scarves or strip, and hardly a bare head amongst all those hundreds of men. This era was the zenith of the millinary trade; Dunn & Co made its name as a hat maker before becoming more generally known as a tailor.

Such was the media interest generated by the meeting between Huddersfield Town and Arsenal in the 1930 FA Cup Final, played on 26th April, that the German propaganda machine swung into action! The Graf Zeppelin was sent to fly low over the ground during the match, and almost overshadowed the event itself. Its first-half appearance seemed to deflect the attention of the Yorkshire team, and the Zeppelin was still overhead when Alec James scored the opening goal in the sixteenth minute. However, Town had no such excuse when Arsenal broke away again to score a second goal two minutes from time, thus securing the first of the team's many FA Cup wins.

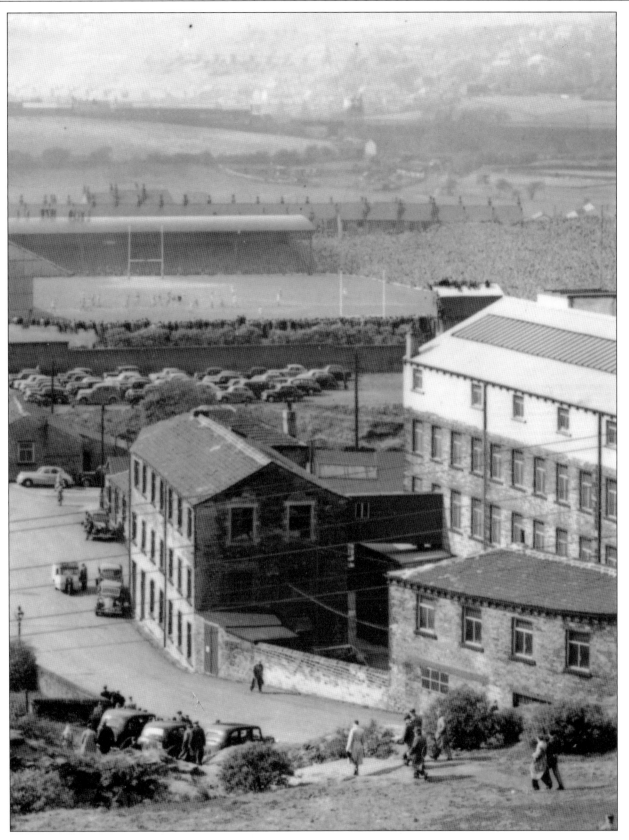

The Rugby League Championship Final, played on 10th May 1952 between Wigan and Bradford Northern, was the first rugby match ever played on the Leeds Road ground. This view from Dalton Bank shows the unusual sight of rugby posts on the pitch, together with a section of the 48,656-strong crowd. Mathematicians will be quick to spot that this makes the crowd 6,344 short of the 55,000 limit - and indeed this point was seized upon by some sections of the Rugby League Press, since thousands of would-be spectators were locked out of the ground. This stadium never again hosted a major rugby final, so Wigan can claim 100 per cent success in major rugby finals played at Leeds Road. They were victors on this occasion by thirteen points to six.

A major fire damaged the Leeds Road stadium on 3rd April, 1950. The main stand was gutted, though the original sub-structure of 1910 survived and still held the West Stand until the stadium was demolished in 1994. Following the fire, re-building began immediately; of the three 'home' fixtures which remained to be played that season, two were played at Elland Road, Leeds. By the following September the stand had still not been completely re-built, but spectators were allowed into certain sections. Here we see part of the crowd of 28,645 looking on from the north-west section of the ground during the match with Sheffield Wednesday on 23rd September, 1950. The new tip-up seats were considered very innovative!

Above: This young man was to become one of football's most valuable commodities during the 1960s. The teenage Denis Law was 'discovered' by Huddersfield Town manager Andy Beattie, and made his debut for the club on Christmas Eve 1956 - by which time Beattie had been replaced as manager by Bill Shankley. Barely two months later, contracts had been drawn up and on Monday, 27th February 1957, Denis Law signed for the club. Aged just 17, he was the youngest professional player in the football league at that time. He was not destined to wear the blue and white shirt for long, however; in 1960 Manchester City made Huddersfield Town an offer they could not refuse, and Denis Law changed hands for £55,000. This was the highest price ever paid for a player by a British club, although three years earlier Leeds United had sold their Welsh international John Charles to Juventus for £65,000. This marked the beginning of an era of clubs paying what some people might call 'silly money' in transfer fees, and, perhaps rather sadly, Denis Law is remembered as much for the huge sums of money he fetched as for his outstanding playing ability. In 1961 he commanded another record transfer fee when Manchester City sold him to Torino for £100,000 - and he appreciated in value so much during the year he spent over there that when Manchester City's old rivals Manchester United decided they wanted him, they had to fork out a cool £115,000.

Both pictures: Cricket enthusiasts have always enjoyed the game of deciding which was the greatest English test side of all time. Most votes have probably been cast for the team which flourished at the turn of the last century, the 'Golden Age', as it is sometimes called, full of glamorous figures: Archie MacLaren, the skipper, whose 424 for Lancashire versus Somerset remains the highest score made by an English player; CB Fry, who was offered the throne of Albania; Ranjitsinhji, the Indian prince with the silky batsmanship; Gilbert Jessop, the big hitter who was an early forerunner of Ian Botham. But equally important to the success of this side was our famous duo from Kirkheaton. George Hirst and Wilfred Rhodes were pillars of Yorkshire and England cricket. Both were exceptional all-rounders; both of them bowled left-handed and batted righthanded.

In our photograph we see Hirst frozen in the awkward pose that the camera of the day required of bowlers - no dynamic action photos then! But he was in fact quite quick, whereas Rhodes was a slow bowler in the classic mould.

Between them, in first class cricket, they scored 76,000 runs and took nearly 7,000 wickets. They had some glory days in Test matches too.

They were together at the crease when England beat Australia by one wicket in one of the legendary Test matches - the last game of the 1902 series at the Oval. Earlier in the same series, they took all ten wickets between them at Edgbaston when the Australians were bowled out for a humiliating 36.

They did as much as anyone to establish Yorkshire as the premier county in English cricket. Shrewd, tough, and masters of their craft, they were still playing first class cricket after the age of 50 - none of the premature 'burn-out' of the modern professional sportsman here. Wilfred Rhodes, in fact, was recalled to play his last Test at the age of 49, and did so with distinction. Rhodes was also remarkable for the fact that he began his playing career batting at number 11, but eventually opened for his country.

Although they seemed to typify gritty Yorkshire professionalism, after the end of their playing days they transferred their skills to a very different setting: the public schoolboys of Eton might have learned something more than just the technique of the square cut when coached by George Hirst, and young men at Harrow will surely have been given an insight into more than the mysteries of slow bowling when they received the benefit of Wilfred Rhodes' long experience.

In more modern times, it became common for sportsmen to go on to become sports commentators at the end of an illustrious career; but in Hirst and Rhodes' day, broadcasters on the wireless were required to use plummy BBC English with cut-glass vowels, so this was not an option for players who spoke with a regional accent.

Memorable
moments

These ladies of assorted ages are preparing to embark on Mr Percy Gee's all-weather coach, which will take them on an outing to Southport. Percy Gee was one of two brothers who both lived in Outlane, and both owned coaches. The all-weather coach seen in this marvellous photograph was an ingenious vehicle with a removable roof which could be pulled all the way forward to provide full cover, or could be rolled back over a series of hoops to let the sunshine in. A decade or so earlier during the 1920s, tyres were still solid and our ladies would have had a rather bumpier ride, but luckily for them their coach was likely to have pneumatic tyres. The ladies seem to be well protected against the cold, with fur collars and stoles much in evidence. One wonders how many of those hats will stay on in the wind if the coach goes topless - though coaches of that vintage were very unlikely to exceed 25 miles an hour. This may seem intolerably slow to us, but in 1928 a motoring publication entitled The Light Car & Cyclecar expressed the view that an average speed of 20 miles per hour over a journey of a reasonable length was the most anybody had any right to expect - though it did concede that an experienced motorist driving a sports car could hope to average 30 miles per hour.

Left: These happy, cheeky faces are clearly off on an expedition of some kind. When a bus or coach is chartered for a special outing, the fun begins as soon as the coach sets off, and the spirit of camaraderie lasts until it arrives back. Before it became usual for families to have at least one car, and to chauffeur their children to school, to friends' houses, to out-of-school activities and so on, children used to spend much more of their time on buses. Some of the older buses on the school run used to have long bench seats upstairs, with the stairs at the back and one corridor running down the side of the upper deck - this was great fun if you felt like getting up to mischief, such as throwing paper aeroplanes, as when the bench seats were packed full the conductor could not easily see who the mischief-makers were. On service buses, the rule for many years was that smoking was permitted upstairs but not downstairs. This gave the upper deck a certain allure for rebellious adolescents; even if you didn't smoke, you could get a little rowdy without attracting disapproving looks from the primmer passengers who preferred the lower deck. And if you did enjoy the occasional fag yourself, and your parents noticed that your hair and clothes smelt of cigarette smoke, you always had an alibi; you just had to make the excuse that there had been no seats downstairs on the bus, so you'd had to go upstairs. Though we can't imagine that the innocent faces pictured here could ever stoop to that kind of behaviour....

Above: Mr Chambers, a well-known instructor in the period between the two world wars, is seen here presiding over the Holmfirth and District Life-Saving Class, which in 1937 included young Morris Bray, lying prostrate nearest the camera; Morris went on to run a successful photographic studio in town. The class took place at Holmfirth Lido, at Hope Bank Pleasure Ground. Hope Bank was situated at Honley, where Brook Motors now are, and up to the second world war it used to be a popular place for family days out, with all kinds of dare-devil attractions arranged for the youngsters. Post-war Town Guides make no mention of it, so we assume it did not re-open after the war. The lads pictured would have been too young for National Service when on 27th April 1939 - 18 weeks before Britain officially declared war on Germany - the first batch of call-up papers were sent out to men aged 20 and 21. However, youngsters could join cadet organisations, women joined the WVS or the ATS, the ARP needed all the volunteers it could get, men aged between 17 and 65 were wanted in the LDV (Local Defence Volunteers - unkindly nicknamed the Look, Duck and Vanish brigade, and later renamed the Home Guard), and there was plenty of war work for everyone. The category of people required to register for war work was at one stage extended to include women aged between 46 and 50 - but of all the measures introduced by Mr Ernest Bevin, Minister of Labour and National Service, calling up grannies for war work was perhaps one of the least popular.

Left: The year is 1949, and the tragic consequences of war are very much at the forefront of everyone's mind as the solemn procession makes its way through Greenhead Park on Fallen Heroes Memorial Day. This annual ceremony was instituted in 1905, in commemoration of the soldiers who had fallen in the Boer War. The original Fallen Heroes Memorial in the park, dedicated to volunteer and regular soldiers who had lost their lives in the South African War, was unveiled in 1905 by General French. Within the space of less than half a century the ranks of Huddersfield's fallen heroes had been swelled by those killed in action in two world wars. The Cenotaph was erected to commemorate the victims of the first world war, and was unveiled on 26th April, 1924. In due course a new plaque was added for those killed in the second world war, and unveiled on Fallen Heroes Day, 23rd May, 1948. The ceremony pictured here took place just one year later. Fallen Heroes Day was subsequently combined with Remembrance Day and commemorated in November. As time passed, the links with the Boer War were lost; looking back at the records it appears that November 1953 was the first occasion on which there was no member of the Huddersfield South African War Veterans' Association present at the Remembrance Day service. It was bitterly cold that day and common sense dictated that no war veteran should be exposed to such weather, and so the Association's wreath was laid on their behalf by a member of the British Legion.

Below: Spectators have gathered to watch the procession march through Greenhead Park on 22nd May, 1949 - Fallen Heroes Day. The full range of Huddersfield's military and civilian organisations were represented in the parade. However solemn the occasion might be, nevertheless there is always something exciting about the sight of so many smart uniforms with all the gleaming buttons, buckles and badges, and the tramp of so many thousands of feet marching in step to the accompanying bands. Parades had been a regular feature of the war years, when they were seen as a valuable means of raising morale and helping the British public feel in touch with the troops - as well as encouraging recruitment. So virtually every uniformed organisation, including the WVS, the cadets and even the nurses, was well-drilled in parade ground technique - 'square-bashing', as it was called - and took its turn at marching through the streets, doing its bit to raise the spirits of the nation. In the section of the procession captured on this snapshot we see some of the younger participants - Girl Guides, followed by Sea Cadets. The war had been over for four years and things were slowly getting back to normal, but rationing was not over yet. However, in the year of this photograph the little children seen here would at least be able go to a shop and buy sweets without a ration coupon, for the first time in their lives.

Thrillers, comedies, musicals, romances, war films, westerns, cartoons - the ABC Ritz had 'em all. One of the films on offer here was 'What Lola Wants', a musical directed by Stanley Donen and George Abbot - a team perhaps more famous for its production of 'Singin' in the Rain', starring Gene Kelly. 'What Lola Wants' was the British title of the film released in America as 'Damn Yankees'; the English title was derived from one of the songs in it, 'Whatever Lola Wants'. This was an era when the American film industry dominated our cinema screens, and 'What Lola Wants' was about as American as a film can get. The story is set in New York and is about America's national sport, baseball.

In fact, 'Damn Yankees' was a hit on Broadway before being transferred to the silver screen, along with most of the cast - though Tab Hunter, who will probably be best remembered for his number one hit record 'Young Love' in 1957, was brought in to take the lead role in the film version. 'What Lola Wants' was a colourful, glittering musical comedy with plenty of good tunes and a satirical edge. The story is basically a combination of the Faust legend and a novel by Douglas Wallop entitled 'The Year The Yankees Lost The Pennant'. It tells the story of a baseball fan who says he would give up his soul if only his team, the Washington Senators, could have a chance to beat the New York Yankees. Enter Satan ...

Below: The sight of happy cinema-goers spilling out of the Ritz, or queuing up to get in, used to be a common sight in Market Street. The Ritz Picture Theatre was built in 1936 on the site of Huddersfield's Cloth Hall. With a seating capacity of two thousand, it was used as a concert venue as well as a cinema, and could be hired for special occasions; for instance, ICI used to book a special showing for its annual kiddies' Christmas Treat. A visit to the flicks was popular with every age group. Many of today's married couples will remember films they watched at the Ritz in their courting days, holding hands shyly on the back row. Possibly they saw Huddersfield's own star of the silver screen in action here: James Mason, the son of a Huddersfield textile merchant, was born in Marsh in 1909. But by 1960 television was beginning to have a major impact on the nation's entertainment habits, and cinemas found it increasingly difficult to tempt people out of their armchairs. In 1960 there were 10.5 million television sets in

Britain, and by 1968 there were 19 million. Many cinemas split their single large auditorium into two or three smaller ones, to offer a choice of viewing, but even so they failed to attract sufficient numbers and many cinemas were forced to shut down. The ABC Ritz was split into two screens and clung on for longer than many, but in December 1982 numbers had dropped to a point where the cinema was no longer viable, and it was announced that the ABC would close the following March. The site was subsequently occupied by Sainsburys.

Bottom: For the coronation of Queen Elizabeth II, we put out the flags, held parties, bought souvenirs - and decorated our buses. This pre-war trolley-bus was given a special red, white and blue livery, with upper and lower deck panels further adorned with flags, a varied array of shields, and even a portrait of Her Majesty the Queen. The pretty young Princess had already won our hearts for her

courage during the war, when she spoke out bravely on the radio with her message for the nation's children. So we bought all kinds of souvenirs of the occasion - spoons, mugs, plaques, brooches, hankies, headsquares, and even hat-pins with small crowns at the end. Every child received a gift valued at around one shilling from the Education Committee: the under-elevens were given a coronation spoon and a book, boys over eleven got a coronation pocket knife, and girls over eleven got a special coronation spoon, of better quality than the one given to the younger ones. Televising the coronation of Elizabeth II made broadcasting history, and must have converted many viewers to this new medium. It was less than two years since Holme Moss transmitter had first come on air, amidst great publicity, at 10am on 15th August, 1951, and very few people actually had a television set.

This fancy dress parade is part of Meltham Co-op's Field Day and Gala celebrations in 1953. Cowboys and Indians are a popular theme, along with a few pirates, and a young Queen is dashing along holding her crown on. It is a lively and heart-warming scene. Meltham Co-op was an institution with a great tradition behind it, and made an immense contribution to community life in many ways. At one time there were two branches of the Co-operative movement active in Meltham: Meltham Mills Provident Co-operative Trading Society Limited, and Meltham Industrial Co-operative Trading Society Limited. The two were amalgamated in 1927. The Meltham Mills movement was the older of the two, having been formed in 1827. There is evidence that Meltham Mills was the first Co-operative Society to pay dividends on purchases, although the Rochdale Pioneers are more commonly credited with this. The truth seems to be that Co-operative Societies were springing up all over Britain, all operating independently but all committed to the same ideals. In later years, of course, 'divi' became one of the Co-op's great attractions. Many families saved up their divi to pay for the annual holiday, and the family's divi number was permanently etched into the memories of even its youngest member, to be quoted whenever they made any purchase, however small - it all added up! In 1949 the Co-op National Membership Scheme was launched. This meant that Co-op members qualified for divi on purchases from any Co-operative Society, not just their own - as one slogan put it: 'She shall have divi wherever she goes!' But as high street retailing became big business, Co-ops struggled to compete with cut-price supermarkets, and Meltham Co-operative Society closed down in 1969.

Right: This photograph was taken in July 1953 at Meltham Mills Carnival; the crowd is clearly waiting for part of the procession to pass by. The post-war period brought prosperity to Meltham Mills. David Brown's tractor factory had been established in the Mills, which prior to that had been the textile mills of Jonas Brook Bros. Having sent a tractor for exhibition at the 1939 Royal Show, the David Brown factory was then turned to gear manufacture for the war effort, although it did make a few tractor vehicles for aircraft towing and recovery. In 1946 the factory switched to the work it had been designed for, producing farm tractors which were exported all over the world. The business expanded, and two years after this photograph it took over the rival firm of Harrison, McGregor & Guest Ltd, of Leigh. But the good times did not last. As the 20th century progressed, bits of Meltham's village life disappeared. The demise of Meltham Co-op was a sad loss, as the Co-op had been there as long as anyone could remember, and provided employment. However, possibly the most difficult time for Meltham was the period during the 1980s when Browns had to close down their Meltham factory; this came shortly after the closure of Shaws packaging factory, and a village which had had plentiful employment suddenly found itself with virtually none.

Below: Towns and villages all over Britain spent months planning and organising their celebrations for the coronation of Queen Elizabeth II. It was a time for families and communities to celebrate together. Streets, shops and houses were decorated with flags and bunting, and above all everybody did their utmost to make sure it was a special occasion for the children. And if there's one thing guaranteed to go down well with kids, it's a fancy dress contest! First there's the excitement of deciding what to be, and then there's the fun of making the costume. The post-war years were the heyday of the Singer sewing machine; most mothers either had one or knew someone who had, so, with a little skill and a lot of imagination, bits of material from the rag-bag could be turned into marvellous outfits - as demonstrated on stage here. This jolly bunch was photographed at Emley. Another highlight of Emley's coronation celebrations was a procession of historical tableaux which included one float designed to represent the New Elizabethan Age, featuring a group of young people enjoying the anticipated glories of the new Queen's reign. A tableau such as this, at a time when rebuilding the country's economy after the war was still top priority, must have encouraged onlookers to picture in their own minds the peaceful, happier and more prosperous times which lay ahead. Half a century or so later, we are tempted to wonder just what their vision of the future consisted of, and whether their dreams were realised.

As we can see, Park Road Methodist Church, which before its demolition occupied the spot where Crosland Moor Community Centre now stands, got a good turnout to its Primrose Fair on 21st March, 1953. It was a well-planned event. Advance publicity announced that the fair would begin at 3 pm, and there would be stalls, a film show, afternoon tea and public tea (we confess that we are not quite sure what the difference is between the two different kinds of tea; no doubt readers who do know will enlighten us). The Chairman of the Committee was Mr N Hutchinson, Mr Harold Inman was to be the opener, and the soloists were Mary Bottomley, soprano, and Colin Schofield, bass - from which we

astutely deduce that musical entertainment was also on the agenda. Mary Bottomley, later Mary Newman, went on to become choirmistress at Outlane Methodists. Unfortunately we have not been able to track down any details of Park Road Methodists' 1953 Primrose Fair beyond the advance notice and this charming photograph. However, judging from the crowd of people, the table laden with food and decorated with daffodils, and the gay stalls in the background, it had all the ingredients of a successful afternoon which deserved to swell church funds nicely. It is nice to see such a mix of ages amongst the guests: there are children, young couples and older people, all dressed up for the occasion. What a happy picture they make!

Primrose Hill Gala Day, held in July, was the village's annual free treat for the children. In reality, as we all learn sooner or later, nothing good comes for free; so in order to fund the gala, events such as pantomimes and concerts were put on locally over a period of months, with proceeds going towards Gala Day, and collections were also made on the day itself. Here we see part of the fancy dress parade of the 1953 Gala, the year when Miss Joan Matthews was Primrose Hill's Rose Queen. Young imaginations have been busy here! Of course, in coronation year no procession would be complete without at least one queen, and we have a very fine one here complete with ermine robes. In the foreground is a doll's pram reminiscent of

those navy blue Silver Cross prams in which many an infant born within a decade or so of the second world war spent happy baby days. The ingenious lightweight buggies which had taken over by the end of the 20th century had clear advantages, but in their own way the baby carriages of the 1950s and 60s were splendid contraptions, with superb coachwork, robust enough to carry all your heavy shopping as well as your infant. Prams built in the 30s and 40s were actually designed with inbuilt storage under the padded board that Baby lay upon - you took Baby out, lifted up the board, and there you had a capacious compartment where you were supposed to keep extra blankets and bottles, but which you could equally well use for stowing your shopping.

Above: Younger readers may well be astonished to see all these ladies seated round the dinner table with their hats on. In fact, it was perfectly usual for ladies to keep hats on in cafes, even when they took their coats off. In this case, though, everybody has kept their coat on as well; and this, coupled with the fact that it is still too early in the year to cast a clout and all the windows are open, suggests that it was on the chilly side when they sat down to enjoy their Coronation meal at Royds House, Shelley, in May 1953 - but no doubt the hall warmed up as the meal progressed. This was a generation that saw a succession of monarchs come and go. Queen Victoria died in 1901; her son, Edward VII, reigned for just nine years before

dying of pneumonia. His successor, the popular King George V, died in January 1936, shortly after celebrating the 25th anniversary of his accession. Then followed the Mrs Simpson affair and the abdication of Edward VIII. George VI, Edward's shy younger brother, was crowned instead, and won a special place in the hearts of his subjects. No doubt the diners at Royds House were genuinely saddened by his death from lung cancer in 1952. A great many coronation parties and celebrations had been arranged in Huddersfield and throughout the country; and though the occasion pictured here may have been less frivolous than some, no doubt in their hearts they are welcoming the pretty young Queen Elizabeth to the throne.

A few have spotted the camera, but most of the kiddies are too entranced by the Punch and Judy show to even notice that they are having their picture taken. Since they performed to this appreciative audience in Emley as part of the 1953 Coronation celebrations, Punch and Judy have had to clean their act up. Boo, Mr Punch, you can't keep whacking Judy over the head and expect to get away with it! As a society we became much more sensitive about potentially offensive terminology and behaviour during the course of the 20th century. In the early part of the century, freak shows were a popular entertainment, and every circus would have its dwarves, fat ladies, and any other unusually-proportioned humans or animals that they could recruit. As we became more enlightened, we realised how cruel this was to the individuals concerned. It used to be quite acceptable to talk about old age pensioners, until it occurred to us that calling people old is not nice, so we struggled with various euphemisms such as OAPs and Senior Citizens. Some might feel that the list of expressions to be avoided had, by the end of the 20th century, reached ridiculous extremes. Along the same lines, children's literature and entertainment came under scrutiny, to ensure that impressionable young minds were protected from bad influences such as Noddy and Big Ears. There was talk of banning Mr Punch too, but in the end he was allowed to stay - on condition that he behaved himself.

Above: These worthy ladies and gentlemen formed a section of the guests at the Meltham Civic Ball in November 1953. As 1953 drew to a close and the village started looking forward to Christmas, the Council was once again preparing to do its bit towards making Meltham a festive place to be, by providing a Christmas tree. It could not, however, go in its traditional spot in Market Place, because of the alterations in the road layout which had taken place during the course of the year. These included the provision of an elongated traffic island with a bollard; Meltham, in common with other villages and towns throughout the country, had begun to notice an increase in the use of private cars on its roads. Meltham's investment in road safety measures proved farsighted, as the rise in car ownership was to be so dramatic that a decade later, one adult in seven was a car owner. But the new layout of Market Place did mean that there was nowhere to put the tree, and, after some investigation and much careful thought, the Council settled upon a nice corner of Meltham churchyard. So that was where it went, that was where the lighting-up ceremony took place, and afterwards the children of Meltham School stood round the illuminated tree and sang carols.

Above right: Huddersfield is deservedly well known for its thriving and varied musical scene. Each year the Huddersfield Contemporary Music Festival attracts visitors from all over the world. There are numerous excellent local orchestras, brass bands, ensembles, operatic groups, musical societies - and choirs, many of whom are famous far beyond Huddersfield. The best known is probably the Huddersfield Choral, which sets extremely high standards and requires members to re-audition on a regular basis; this used to take the form of individual auditions but is now done section by section, on a three-yearly cycle. Other established and successful choirs at the end of the 20th century included the Huddersfield Methodists Choir which celebrated its Golden Jubilee in 1996, the Holmfirth Choral, the Colne Valley Male Voice Choir and its smaller but very competitive rival the Gledholt Male Voice Choir, and also the Marsh Ladies and the Pennine Singers. Music festivals such as the Harrogate and the Blackpool festivals and annual Mrs Sunderland competition consistently attract many entries and creditable performances from both junior and senior choirs from the Huddersfield area.

Below: Holding their certificates and smiling in delight are students of the Charles Frost School of Dancing. This group of medallists was photographed in January 1954. Huddersfield boasted a good number of dancing schools around that time, and we guess that many readers will have taken lessons at one or another of them - perhaps the Atack School of Dancing, or the Mary Carlton School, or the Hudson School, or Rawlins'; or at Fox's Academy of Dancing on Trinity Street, or the Starlight Dance Studios at 36 Kirkgate. Charles Frost's establishment was at number 9, Brook Street. During the earlier part of the 20th century a number of new dance steps became popular and subsequently became an established part of dance students' repertoire. Some were old dances revived, and some were imported - for instance, there was the Foxtrot, the Rumba, and the Tango, which originated in South America and became all the rage with Britain's gay young things around 1910-1920. The 1950s saw us learning to jive and rock-and-roll, but after that, disco dancing took over in most dance halls, and new dance routines tended to be passing crazes based upon a single hit record. During the 70s we gave ourselves headaches pogoing to punk bands like the Sex Pistols - who incidentally gave their last concert in Huddersfield on Christmas Day 1977. Dancing takes many forms; somehow it's difficult to imagine this group of dancers pogoing the night away dressed in black plastic binliners, with their hair dyed pink and green and cut in a Mohican ...

Bottom: Balloons, party hats and a sea of happy little faces - it must be Christmas. Well, not far off; it is in fact January 1954, and we are at David Brown's children's Christmas Party. All the kiddies are dressed in their best, which generally meant frocks or pinafore dresses and blouses for the girls, and collars and ties for the boys. And in 1954, children had knees; mothers dressed their little girls not in leggings, jog suits or jeans, but in skirts and dresses, and those little white ankle socks that stayed in fashion for many years. Young lads generally wore shorts and long socks until they went to secondary school; as often as not a boy's first pair of trousers came as part of his new school uniform, and suddenly he looked very grown-up. Not until the last generation or so have children been dressed like miniature adults. Little girls had frocks, little boys had shorts, and as often as not children's clothes were handed down and passed around until there was more patch than original material, with no small voices raised to complain that everybody else at school has the latest designer gear and why can't they?

Many villages around the country have lost the picturesque traditions that used to be an important part of village life, but in Huddersfield we had the good sense to preserve and even re-institute a lot of them. Among the more unusual and spectacular folk traditions are Marsden's annual celebration of Imbolc (the pagan fire festival), as well Marsden Cuckoo Day, with Maypole dancing, Morris dancing and all manner of pageantry, while along the valley Slaithwaite still holds its annual Moonraking ceremony. Here we see the good people of Meltham, who have turned out in force to see the band on the occasion of a Meltham Co-op Field Day and Gala during the 1950s. In a village which is home to one of Yorkshire's finest bands, no event could be complete without the rousing sound of trumpets, cornets,

trombones, flugels and the rest. Meltham Mills Band's distinguished history began back in the 19th century. It was founded in 1846, the year after Meltham Mills Church was first dedicated, and around three decades later they achieved the triple, winning the British Open Championship, or the Belle Vue Championship as it was then, three years in a row: 1876, 1877 and 1888. By the end of the 20th century, only two other Yorkshire bands had ever accomplished this feat - the Black Dyke and the Brighouse & Rastrick. Nineteen fifty-two was a particularly auspicious year for Meltham Mills Band, as that was the year in which it first took over Bent House as its headquarters; we understand that this was initially a temporary arrangement, but Bent House remained the bandroom and subsequently became the property of the band.

Bottom: The modern design of the houses reminds us that Rawthorpe is one of the newer residential areas of Huddersfield, but here we see the community engaged in a thoroughly traditional activity - the annual children's treat. In June 1956, the month of our photograph, children did not have televisions and computer games to keep them in their rooms, and summer holidays meant plenty of outside entertainments for them to join in. Summer often meant going away for a fortnight, too, but the destination was more likely to be Scarborough, Blackpool or Bridlington than Spain. In June 1956 Bridlington was the venue for the National Federation of Old Age Pensioners' annual conference, at which the Federation called for pensions to be increased to £3 a week plus a bonus to meet the rising cost of living. Also in that month the Duke of Edinburgh celebrated his 35th birthday, Stirling Moss came second in the Italian Grand Prix, work started on Britain's first stretch of motorway - the Preston by-pass - and Britain carried out an atom test at Monte Bello, causing Australians to be warned against drinking rainwater in case it contained radio-active dust. Such was life in June, 1956.

Right: The ladies of the WVS went to a great deal of trouble in September 1954 to set everything out nicely for their children's party. We assume this event took place in the new WRVS headquarters on Church Street, which was opened in May of the previous year. Clusters of balloons decorate the walls, the long table has been laid very attractively, and we have no doubt that the children enjoyed all kinds of home-baked treats that afternoon. Parties such as this are in a different league from the glitzy affairs at fast-food establishments that had become so popular by the end of the 20th century. In 1954, party fare meant not hamburgers and chips but sandwiches, jellies, trifles and whatever specialities the organisers had up their sleeves. Eating habits changed tremendously during the second half of the 20th century. One influence on this and other aspects of our lives was the younger generation's craze for anything American. This gathered momentum in the 1960s; we watched Westerns and tried to copy the American drawl, we bought American pop records, we adopted Levi and Wrangler jeans in a big way, and we went to Wimpy Bars to drink Coke and eat hamburgers. As the century progressed, modern global transport and communications meant that we became familiar with more and more cultures and went on to adopt some of their customs, and so Huddersfield developed as a multi-cultural society.

Heywood's shop in Rawthorpe is flying the flag, and we believe that this show of patriotism was in fact prompted by a Royal visit - most likely the one in 1949. Rawthorpe was at that time one of Huddersfield's newer suburbs, having become a residential area in the period between the two world wars. Prior to 1920 it consisted of no more than a handful of dwellings clustered around Rawthorpe Hall. During the 1920s and 30s, housing estates, shops and later schools were built. In later years, Rawthorpe's environs altered a good deal, with the creation of the McAlpine Stadium nearby and a succession of retail and industrial parks springing up along the Leeds Road. This building remained the Post Office and was little altered throughout the 20th century - although the advertisement for Wills-Capstan cigarettes disappeared. In 1949, of course, cigarette advertising was not required to carry a Government health warning. Smoking was socially acceptable, even desirable; television personalities were frequently seen with a fag between their lips. When evidence to support the connection between smoking and lung cancer was first announced, it came as a real shock to smokers everywhere, and there was great reluctance to accept the scientists' findings. Yet while the Union Jacks flutter bravely above Rawthorpe Post Office, our monarch - himself a heavy smoker - already has the disease; within a short time he will visibly deteriorate, and in 1952 he will die of lung cancer.

Ben Shaw's pop has been a favourite down the generations, on hot sunny days in the park, holidays by the seaside, parties at home, or galas such as the 1958 ICI Children's Gala seen here. Benjamin Shaw & Sons Ltd was founded in 1871, opened their Willow Lane factory in 1894, and became one of the largest manufacturers of soft drinks and one of Huddersfield's major employers. By 1958, the era was fast approaching when a child's all-time favourite snack would be 'a can of pop and a bag of crisps please'. The year after this photograph was taken, Ben Shaw became the first soft drink manufacturer in Europe to successfully put a fizzy soft drink into a can. Marketed as Suncharm, this was exported all over the world. The company went from strength to strength, opening a site in Oldham in 1964, and the Brockholes factory in 1966. Another novelty drink launched by the company in the 1960s was Space Special, which came in a non-returnable glass bottle, and was especially for children. The price of the bottle of pop generally included a deposit on the bottle, so you always took your empties back to the shop to get your pennies back. Thinking about pop and crisps - how many readers remember the pre-Ready Salted era, when a bag of crisps came with a twist of blue paper inside, containing the salt? They brought the idea back, decades later, as a sales gimmick, but the salt was in a little sealed bag instead of a twist, and it wasn't the same....

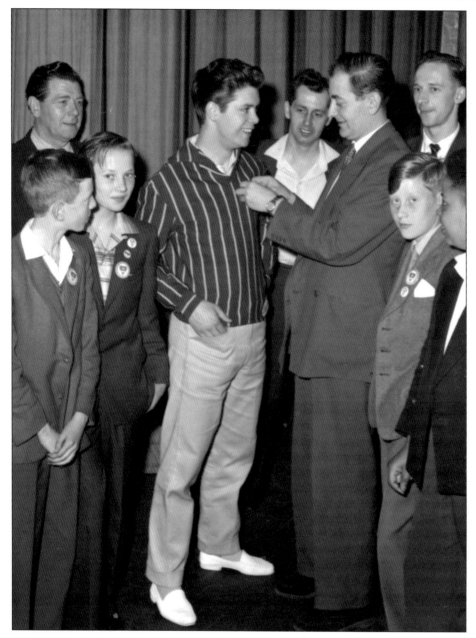

Above: Saturday, 15th May 1959 was the day that all Cliff Richard fans in the Huddersfield area had been waiting for, and here we see the man himself, preparing for a publicity session backstage at the ABC Ritz Cinema. Cliff's first hit record, Move It, had reached Number Two the previous September. Later in 1959 he was to have two Number Ones, Livin' Doll and Travellin' Light, and over the next few years he was to rank as the top British rock 'n' roll star in an era when the charts were dominated by American music. Cliff went on to have more hit records in the UK than anybody except Elvis - more than the Rolling Stones, and considerably more than the Beatles. However, the fresh-faced young man seen here at the beginning of his career had no way of knowing just how phenomenal his success would be, and tickets for his two shows at the Huddersfield ABC Ritz were modestly priced at six shillings, five shillings and four shillings. When Cliff returned to Huddersfield in 1963, this time with The Shadows, fans had to pay more or less double that amount to see him, with tickets at 12/6, 10/- and 7/6. This proved no great deterrent; some teenagers queued all night to make sure of their seats, and all the tickets for both performances were snapped up in advance - a total of 4,072 tickets. Of course the young men who went to the concert could not understand what the girls saw in Cliff; all the lads were interested in was seeing the Shadows, so that they could copy Hank Marvin's unique guitar sound.

The bevy of beauties on-stage has been taking part in the Miss ICI beauty contest at the Town Hall. Their hairdos are immediately reminiscent of the 1960s, and in fact 1963 is given as the date of our photograph. At that time many people's social lives tended to revolve around work to a greater extent than was generally the case by the end of the 20th century. Big local employers such as the Co-op, ICI, Hopkinsons, Broadbents and John Brown would organise a full calendar of social events - dances, beauty contests, works trips, open days, galas, a host of treats for employees' children, and so forth. Firms had their own brass band, their own operatic society, and active

sports teams. These were all seen as perks of working for a big company, and no doubt encouraged staff loyalty; and so of course the presentation of long service awards was another important annual event. In the year that this stunning young lady became Miss ICI, the firm broke with tradition, deciding, after much deliberation, that instead of automatically presenting gold watches to those eligible, they would offer a choice of items such as silver tea sets, canteens of cutlery and silver cigarette cases. The presentation ceremony was held at Whiteley's cafe, and the vote of thanks, given as the proceedings drew to a close, paid tribute to the 'tremendous team spirit' of all the ICI employees.

Ever since the chemical industry started, it has had to contend with the the problem of storing and disposing of hazardous waste. The worst ever fire at the chemical waste tip of Messrs Holliday & Co Ltd broke out on Sunday 25th September 1955, and spectators came from far and wide to see the sight. The fire blazed for around six hours, throwing flames up hundreds of feet into the air, accompanied by black oily smoke and fumes. The glow was reportedly visible from Knottingley, some 26 miles away. At the height of the blaze, molten waste flowed down the tip like lava from a volcano, spreading the fire to properties on Leeds Road. The occupants of four houses, one of them an 86-year-old woman, had to leave their homes, and houses on the Bradley Estate were also evacuated as a precaution. The WVS set up an emergency centre at Deighton Methodist School, where they kept food and drinks on the go, and provided temporary accommodation for those made homeless. The houses on Leeds Road were destroyed in the blaze, and although members of the Huddersfield Round Table, along with Corporation workmen and officials, did their utmost to rescue furniture and possessions from inside the buildings, the unfortunate inhabitants lost many of their belongings. An appeal was promptly launched on their behalf, and numerous items of furniture and other household essentials were donated. Investigations showed that the fire had been started by three youths, who had lit a fire in a tin and dropped it onto the tip.

On the move

To most people, 1914 means the outbreak of World War I. But there were other events of some significance taking place that year too, and one of them was the extension of Huddersfield Corporation's tram network along the Colne Valley to Marsden. This very old photograph was taken on 3rd October 1914, the day on which the route was officially opened, and shows the first tram after its arrival at Marsden. Prior to the laying of the extension, the route had terminated at Slaithwaite, some two and a half miles closer to Huddersfield. The Marsden route linked up with the service to Bradley, making it Huddersfield

Corporation's longest tram route, with a total distance, end to end, of almost eleven miles. Mr Roy Brook records that the through fare from town to Marsden in 1914 was 5d, and the service ran every half hour during weekdays, but at quarter of an hour intervals between 4.30 and 8.30 pm on weekday evenings and for extended periods over the weekend. An attractive village, then as now, Marsden was a popular place to visit, both for itself and as a gateway to Marsden Moors, so at weekends the journey out by tram, running as it did through open countryside, attracted many passengers who were simply enjoying a day out.

Above: A wonderful collection of vehicles has obligingly assembled for the photographer in St George's Square on this day in 1938. There's a tram, a couple of trolley buses, and in the background a Scammel motor wagon. Outside the railway station and the George Hotel there are cars and taxis, and round the corner from the George is a horse and cart. And of course there is always Shanks' pony, which by 1938 had become a very vulnerable form of transport. In the period between the two world wars, a horrifying 120,000 people were killed on Britain's roads. We can see here that Belisha beacons have been installed in St George's square to help pedestrians cross in safety, although striped zebra crossings would not appear in Huddersfield for more than a decade. The principle of the pedestrian crossing was introduced in 1934 as part of Leslie Hore-Belisha's package of measures to improve road safety, which also included the introduction of the 30 mph speed limit in built-up areas. Another potentially hazardous situation during the tram era used to be alighting from a tram at a tram stop. The layout of the track made no provision for the tram to pull in to the side of the road at a stop, and although motor cars were supposed to wait behind them when they stopped, of course there were always some drivers, even then, who were in too much of a hurry!

Above right: Here we see trolley bus number 637, captured on film as it plied route 62 in 1958. Route 62 took it to Fixby, and the bus has stopped by Huddersfield Crematorium - although inexplicably it seems to be on the wrong side of the road. Nineteen fifty-eight was in fact the year in which Huddersfield's new 14-acre crematorium was opened. The total cost of constructing this new facility for the town was in the region of £103,000, and the opening ceremony, performed by Alderman Arthur Gardiner, took place in April of that year. Unfortunately, disaster was to strike a couple of decades or so later; readers who lived in the Fixby area at that time are sure to remember the day in August 1981 when the crematorium was wrecked by a violent explosion, which is reported to have hurled rubble as far as the M62. The building and the grounds were so seriously damaged by the blast, thought to have been caused by a boiler, that the crematorium had to remain closed for more than two years whilst the damage was made good. This inevitably caused some inconvenience and distress to bereaved families, who had to make alternative arrangements. It also meant that pressure was put on neighbouring crematoriums, resulting in some delays. A number of Huddersfield families travelled to Elland crematorium instead during that period. Repairs were carried out as quickly as possible, at a cost of some £5,000, and the crematorium was re-dedicated and re-opened in November 1983.

Below: Trolley bus number 531 is seen here turning into Kirkgate from Castlegate as it travels the route from Waterloo to Outlane; this was the last route to be taken over by the motor buses, and some readers are sure to have been amongst the thousands who watched or travelled on Huddersfield's very last trolley bus, which was decorated and illuminated for the occasion. The vehicle seen here was acquired new in June 1939, and was one of the last batch of pre-war trolley buses to be purchased by Huddersfield Corporation. Road users had to become much more safety-conscious as the 20th century progressed and our roads became busier. This was reflected in vehicle design, in road layout and in a succession of legislative measures which were introduced to tighten up on motorists. The driving test was introduced in 1935, initially on a voluntary basis and then made compulsory for everybody who had taken out their first driving licence after 1st April 1934; anybody who had begun driving prior to that date was not compelled to take a test. Other safety measures included new tyre laws which specified the minimum legal tread, the introduction of the MoT test, and the compulsory wearing of seatbelts - remember when Jimmy Saville used to hammer home the message, from roadside posters and from our television screens: 'Clunk, Click, Every Trip'?

Bottom: Traffic, in our opinion, was much more picturesque in 1937, when this photograph was taken in Railway Street. The type of trams seen here, with a short roof on top leaving each end of the upper deck open to the elements, were nicknamed 'turret cars', and although they make a very charming picture, passengers who had to travel on the exposed sections in bad weather when the tram was full used to arrive at their destination very cold and dripping wet. Beneath the Union Jack, we can see a uniformed Huddersfield Corporation Tramways' employee turning the trolley with his bamboo pole. This little ritual was performed each time a tram reached its terminus, so that it could then

travel in the opposite direction. Some tram operators used a system whereby the overhead trolley wires were designed in such a way as to turn the trolley automatically, but this was never introduced in Huddersfield. Before the introduction of trolley buses into the Huddersfield Corporation transport system, trams on route 7 used to run through from West Vale to Almondbury via the town centre. However, by the time of this photograph the section between town and Almondbury had been taken over by trolley buses. For years the route was split into two, with trams running between West Vale and the terminus in Railway Street, and trolley buses running between town and Almondbury, until on 28 May 1939 the West Vale section too was taken over by trolley buses.

The date of this photograph was 1st May, 1937 - long before there was any need for towns to have ring roads - and the location was the top of Chapel Hill, at the beginning of Manchester Road. The Co-op's extension at the corner of East Parade and Buxton Road (subsequently renamed New Street) was still very new when this snapshot was taken, having been completed the previous year. May 1st, 1937, was in fact the last day of the tram service to Newsome, and in the background we can see a tramcar from Newsome passing the Co-op building. The two tramcars in the foreground are headed for the Colne Valley; one is an old 'turret car', while the other is a newer type with a completely enclosed upper deck. A number of these were trans-ferred to Sunderland when Huddersfield had no further use for tramcars. We understand that later on, when Sunderland stopped running trams, Huddersfield was given an opportunity to have one back free of charge apart from the cost of transporting it; however, this offer was never taken up, so we only have photographs such as this one to remind us of what they used to look like. The Corporation had acquired its first trolley buses in 1933, and was phasing them in route by route. The conversion was a major engineering task, and on some routes, in addition to installing overhead cabling and taking up tram lines, alterations had to be made to the road layout. In such cases, motor buses were used temporarily to keep the service going whilst roadworks were carried out.

Below: Huddersfield Corporation introduced trolley buses on the service between Almondbury and town in December 1933. For a year prior to that, a temporary motor bus service had operated on this route. The track on this route had become worn out, and a decision was taken early in 1932 that instead of re-laying the tram track, at an estimated cost of around £13,000, the route should instead be converted for trolley buses. As successive sections of the track were taken up during the conversion, motor buses operated by the Joint Omnibus Committee were brought temporarily to keep the service going. The last section of tram track to remain operational ran as far as Rookery Road, and along this stretch the last tram ran in April 1933. From then on, motor buses covered the entire stretch until the trolley buses started running in December of that year. Huddersfield Corporation initially bought six prototype trolley buses, of which Number 6, shown here, was the only AEC vehicle. Of the other five, four were built in Huddersfield by Karrier Motors Ltd, who until 1935 were a major employer in the town. Huddersfield opted for six-wheeled trolley buses because during the 1930s the six-wheelers were able to carry more passengers than the early four-wheeled versions. Later on, the carrying capacity of four-wheelers increased, but Huddersfield Corporation continued to run six-wheelers.

Above: Even 21st century technology has no answer to the elements. The M62 has not solved the problem of snow; it, too, can become impassable, and so crossing the Pennines in bad weather remains a major challenge. The combination of steep gradients and high, exposed stretches of road, well above the snow line, have resulted in many scenes such as this, and no doubt many similar scenes still lie ahead for us in the future. This photograph was taken in February 1947. The men wielding the shovels are Polish troops, who are doing a grand job in unblocking the A62 at Standedge. These lorries had been stranded for days when snow blocked the trunk road, which, before the construction of the motorway, was the main route between Huddersfield and Manchester. Standedge is barely ten miles from the centre of Huddersfield, but when the bad weather sets in it can be a desolate and frightening place for solitary motorists. When the official advice to motorists is not to travel unless your journey is absolutely necessary, it is wise to heed the warning and stay at home.

Above right: There is a timeless quality about this scene at Standedge ... Each year, as winter sets in and the skies turn black, cross-Pennine commuters begin to wonder what the coming months will bring. This photograph was taken during the early months of 1953. Snowfalls had deposited snow more than a foot deep in many places, and Standedge Cutting - always one of the worst affected spots - was blocked for a week. We assume that our lone, brave motorist has returned to this desolate scene to dig his vehicle out. Chaos arrived on Tuesday February 10th that year, when blizzards resulted in 50 or more vehicles, including HGVs and private cars, becoming stranded, most between the Great Western Hotel on the Marsden side of the moors and the Horse and Jockey on the Oldham side. Motorists and police battled against the odds in an icy gale and howling winds. And, to make things worse, it was the wrong kind of snow; officials confirmed afterwards it was very wet snow, and therefore harder to shift. Among vehicles stuck on the A62 were at least three bread vans, delivering from Lancashire bakeries to shops in the Huddersfield area. An estimated 6,000 loaves of bread were waiting to get through - and get through they did. Grocers this side the Pennines got their bread, though in some cases it did not arrive until nine o'clock that night. At least it had been kept cool and fresh whilst in transit....

Nostalgic **HUDDERSFIELD**

In July 1955 the Huddersfield Corporation trolley bus service to Brighouse via Rastrick was replaced by motor buses. This view shows the last trolley bus at Brighouse, with the last passengers on the right and a group of trolley bus enthusiasts standing with the driver and conductor on the left. The Brighouse route had been the last route to be converted from trams to trolley buses, with Huddersfield's very last tram running to Brighouse on Saturday 29th June, 1940. Thereafter trolley buses continued to serve this route for just over 15 years. At Brighouse, the trolley buses had to reverse up Bonegate to turn round - a manoeuvre which would surely never be permitted these days. For the first five years that trolley buses plied the Brighouse via Rastrick route, the country was at war. The vehicle seen here is a post-war acquisition, built, we are informed, in 1948. In general, it was considered that vehicles constructed immediately after the war were by and large not ideal and a number of them were subsequently re-bodied. One problem was that there was no opening front window in the upper deck, which led to poor air circulation. The solution was to modify them by putting in a small hinged window, as on the vehicle pictured here. Later vehicles were built with two front windows incorporating sliding panes.

Bottom: The sign on the front of the locomotive leaves us in no doubt about the occasion pictured here. This is in fact one of two special trains which have been chartered by the Huddersfield engineering company Thomas Broadbent & Sons Ltd to take its employees and their families to Butlin's Holiday Camp in Filey, to celebrate the company's centenary. To a modern observer, it seems a little odd that the men are setting off to Butlin's wearing ties, but that was the way in the 1960s; designer casualwear was not an option. The ladies' skirts are still modestly covering the knees, but before long fashions were to become more extreme. The older generation could only look on in horror as their sons wore flowery shirts and grew their hair down past their collar, and their daughters wore shorter and shorter skirts, teamed up with knee-high 'wet-look' boots. It was the new man-made fibres which made these fashions possible; nylon tights allowed hemlines to rise without exposing stocking tops and suspenders, and the 'wet-look' was possible courtesy of the invention of stretch vinyl. By the end of the 60s midi-skirts and maxi-skirts were given an enthusiastic welcome by those of us whose legs were quite frankly not designed to wear minis. Britain's Mary Quant had by that time made her mark on the international fashion scene, earning herself an OBE in 1966 - and in that same year, Thomas Broadbent & Sons Ltd was awarded the Queen's Award for Industry.

Right: Whoops! Trolley bus number 634 has had a mishap at Longwood. The procedure for turning round at the Longwood terminus involved reversing onto a terminal platform, built for that purpose. Originally there had been a turntable here, and the buses used to be driven onto the turntable and winched round by hand, but when the winding mechanism became worn out from constant use it was not replaced. The turntable was removed and a platform was constructed for the buses to reverse onto instead. Unfortunately this one missed and landed in an adjoining field. A large crane has succeeded in lifting it out of the field to be towed away, and the scene has inevitably attracted quite a little knot of spectators. This was in fact the end of trolley bus number 634's short life. It was actually one of Huddersfield Corporation's newest trolley buses, but at the time of this incident on Monday 13th (unlucky for some) February 1967, the days of Huddersfield's trolley bus network were already numbered. In view of this, the bus was judged to be beyond economic repair, and was scrapped.

Making a living

To those of us accustomed to eating our meals surrounded by plush 21st century comforts, the 1950s works canteen at Moxon's Mill might look a little basic. But in the less consumer-orientated days just after the end of the second world war, employees really appreciated facilities such as this - somewhere to get a good, wholesome meal, often at a price subsidised by the company. The Kirkburton firm of BH Moxon was founded in 1887, and in 1950 it moved from Springfield Mill to a newly-built, modern, well-equipped, air-conditioned factory at Southfield Mills. Moxon's, later taken over by Thomas Birkhead, specialised in manufacturing high-quality, stylish, fancy worsteds. The most striking thing about this photograph is the way the sexes have segregated themselves, with the men apparently finding safety in numbers as they huddle around the three tables in the corner. Perhaps we really were more shy, in the days before - as some might say - we picked up the free-and-easy manners from across the Atlantic. Certainly we had a more formal code which dictated how we dressed and how we addressed people. First names were almost never used in a work situation; a boss would always call his secretary Miss or Mrs So-and-so, and she would call him Mr So-and-so, however long they had worked together. By the end of the 20th century, modern PR techniques had changed all that, and to those of us who had spent all our working lives with the old conventions, it came as rather a shock to suddenly find ourselves on first-name terms with strange young men half our age.

Left: This charming snapshot shows a group of trainee nurses, complete with dog, outside the nurses' hostel in Edgerton. We believe that the hostel was Ellersley House on Blacker Road, opposite the cemetery. Government after government failed to find the magic formula to provide the country with an adequate supply of nurses, and one attempt to increase their numbers during the mid-20th century included making revisions to nurse training so that qualifications could be obtained more quickly. Nursing requires not only professional skills, but also very special personal qualities, including the ability to care for people without becoming too emotionally involved. Few things can be potentially more distressing than watching a child fighting for its life against the odds. Fortunately, a great deal of progress was made during the 20th century, particularly in the post-war years, in developing vaccines and controlling infectious diseases. In 1949, ten people died in a polio epidemic which hit the Huddersfield area. Ten cases of polio were reported in 1955, the year of our photograph. By this time, however, scientists were well on the way to developing a vaccine which would successfully protect children from this killer disease. As soon as trials were completed and it was made known to the public that the polio vaccine would shortly be available, parents queued up to put their children's names down for a vaccination. A couple of months later, the first delivery of the new vaccine was received in Huddersfield, and the vaccination programme that was to save countless lives began.

Below: Real ale enthusiasts were saddened when the long-established Lockwood Brewery ceased brewing. The business was founded in 1795 by Timothy Bentley, and will be remembered by most people as Bentley & Shaw's Brewery. Ales were brewed at Lockwood using water from the River Holme, which was regarded as being exceptionally good water; and the brewery is reputed to have been the first to use the Yorkshire stone square system of fermentation, developed by Dr Priestley. The business flourished, and certainly many of our readers will have fond memories of the Town Ales they consumed in their youth. Unfortunately, like countless other small and medium-sized local breweries, Bentley & Shaw were unable to compete when the brewing industry became a battlefield for the giants during the mid-20th century, and the final brew was made at Lockwood in November 1962. A decade later, in 1972, CAMRA - the Campaign for Real Ale - was launched in an attempt to rekindle interest in traditional ale. The campaign was very successful, and over the years it has done a great deal to encourage small breweries. Certainly real ale is alive and well in Huddersfield, and one highly respected real ale pub can be found just a couple of miles away from Lockwood, in Linthwaite, where the Sair Inn serves its tremendous range of Linfit ales including Leadboiler, Old Eli and Enoch's Hammer.

A *lifetime of education*

The origins of Further Education in Huddersfield can be traced back to 1825 with the formation of the Huddersfield Scientific and Mechanics Institute. Although this venture unfortunately failed through lack of support and financial difficulties, there was an obvious need to provide education and training for the boys and young men employed in the local industries, shops and warehouses. The Young Men's Mutual Improvement Society was formed in 1841 and within two years had merged with the Huddersfield Mechanics Institution.

Over the next 150 years the institution continued to develop, expand and reinvent itself through a number of incarnations. The Mechanics Institution moved to premises on Queen Street South in 1884. Fifty years or so since the first development of an institution for Further Education in Huddersfield, the Mechanics Institution became a Technical College in 1896. Eight years later in 1903, the responsibility for management of the College was taken over by Huddersfield Borough Council.

The Technical College flourished in the first half of the century. By the start of the first world war the institution was educating over 1,800 students on a range of courses from day release apprentice training to higher education. The war stimulated growth at the College, largely due to the increased industrial demand in the chemical and dye industries. Similarly the second world war saw an increase in numbers, including trainee teachers evacuated from London, civilians and forces personnel learning basic craft skills.

In the early 1950s the proposal was made by the Ministry of Education to effectively divide the Technical College into two separate institutions. Partly as a result of the increasing growth of the College and partly in response to national policies encouraging the designation of specific institutions for more advanced work, the Ministry proposed that a 'Branch College' be set up in the town for what was then described as 'lower-level work'. The Local Education Authority (LEA) resolved to find accommodation for the Branch College for Junior students. During this period the Technical College became known as Huddersfield College of Technology and the LEA included accommodation for the proposed Branch College in its plans for the Queensgate site (now occupied by the University).

Eventually the Branch College was set up in 1963 using shared accommodation with the College of Technology and with a staff largely transferred from the same institution. The difficult issue of a name for the new College then raised its head. The College had become known locally as The Tech'. Huddersfield College of Education (FE) was established at Lindley and the secondary school at Salendine Nook was known as Huddersfield New College. The Local Education Authority decided on the distinctive title of 'Ramsden Technical College' as a result of the Ramsden family's historic association with the town. Unfortunately this also lead to enquiries as to the location of the town of Ramsden in Yorkshire.

Throughout the 60s the Huddersfield College of Technology and the Ramsden Technical College shared resources, accommodation and equipment as well as staff. The College of Technology continued to develop higher level courses and

Below: *Craft workshop during the 1950s.*

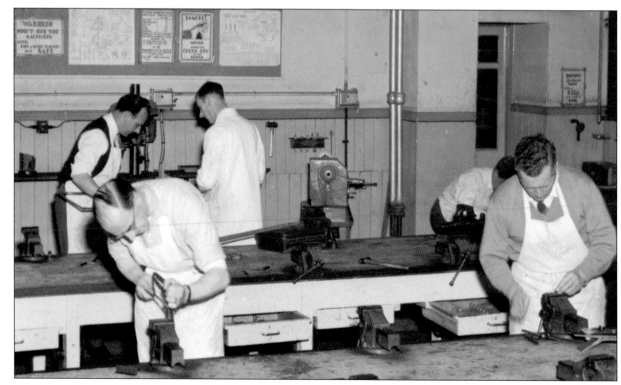

College was offering a wider range of courses in Mechanical and Electrical Engineering, Sciences, Business, Art & Design and GCSE 'O' and 'A' Level subjects and the numbers of students had increased in line. A total of 4,165 students were enrolled for the first year of the College's existence in 1963, increasing to 7,549 by 1971.

The first independent Principal of the new Ramsden Technical College was appointed in 1965. Dr HT Taylor took this post with clear imperative to resolve the problems over accommodation. In 1965 the Royal Infirmary moved to its current location at Lindley leaving the old New North Road site vacant. The LEA sought approval from the Department of Education and Science and the site was transferred from the

with this came an increased demand for accommodation. Originally established with three departments, Engineering, General Studies and Science, the Ramsden Technical College was located in the 'Old Building' on Queensgate which was soon renamed 'The Ramsden Building' - a name which is still in use today. This was far from adequate and the new College was forced to find extra accommodation, where it could, throughout the town. During the academic year 1967-68, the Ramsden Technical College offered courses at over a dozen different locations including Colne Road, Dundas Street and Market Street.

Growth was rapid and new courses were quickly established alongside the phased transfer of courses from the College of Technology. In June 1970 the Huddersfield College of Technology became a Polytechnic and the remaining lower level courses were taken over by the Ramsden Technical College. By the end of the decade the Ramsden Technical

Ministry of Health in I 967. After a programme of refurbishment, Dr Taylor was able to move staff and students into the new premises in September 1968. This relocation helped in the establishment of a separate identity for the College. Following the recreation of the College of Technology into the Polytechnic, the way was clear for consideration of the name of the 'Junior College'. The College Academic Board proposed a reversion to the old name used between 1896 and 1958 and in 1971 the Governors approved the name 'Huddersfield Technical College'.

The New North Road site enabled the College to consolidate most provision in one place and had the added benefit of sufficient land for additional building. This took place in phases over the next 15 years with major construction work providing new accommodation for engineering, science, construction and student services. Despite this, the College continued to use other buildings away from the New North Road campus as annexes including the Highfields site, buildings at Colne Road, St. John's Road and Carr Green Lane and later Taylor Hill Annexe and Brunel House.

Above left: *Flower arranging.*
Top: *Gym class.*

In 1973, local secondary schools were reorganised on comprehensive lines, effectively creating three sixth form colleges in the town. Although competing for students in certain programme areas, there has been significant co-operation between Huddersfield New College, Greenhead College and Huddersfield Technical College, which continues today. The College expanded the range of its provision in the traditional academic areas of GCE '0' Levels (GCSEs) and 'A' Levels, making these programmes available to school leavers and adults.

During the late 1970s the national and local economy deteriorated, resulting in increased redundancies and reduced vacancies. The unemployment rate in Huddersfield increased from 3.8 per cent in December 1978 to 12.6 pe cent in January 1981. During this period there was an increase in student numbers at the College. Many who, in better economic times, might have found employment after leaving school, stayed on in full time education. Many of those who were out of work attended classes to improve their employment prospects. DHSS regulations allowed unemployed people to enrol under certain conditions and the College was permitted to waive their course fees. Throughout this period, the College attempted to anticipate and meet the developing needs of the different communities it served, including the business and industrial sectors. The Manpower Services Commission was also significant during this time and the College expended considerable efforts in establishing training programmes to meet the requirements of the various schemes, such as YTS or Youth Training Scheme.

Following the retirement of Dr Taylor in 1990, the College appointed Dr Malcolm Rossiter as Principal. Dr Rossiter was instrumental in guiding Huddersfield Technical College through the difficult period of incorporation, overseeing the transfer from the local authority to its current status as an educational charitable trust. The College was able to evolve into a secure and successful independent organisation and did so without the internal conflicts and disputes that affected many other further education institutions in this period. The incorporation of the College marked the start of a very different environment for the staff. From being a part of the local metropolitan council and sharing many central services and administrative functions, the College had to develop systems and engage staff to manage finance and payroll, buildings, health and safety, caretaking and cleaning and many other functions.

Above: *Car maintenance in the 1970s.*
Right: *Construction of new facilities at the new North Road site.*

At the same time, the source of funding changed from being the LEA to a new national organisation the Further Education Funding Council (FEFC). The FEFC operated a complex funding methodology. This made possible a degree of central control over the operations of Colleges by giving certain operations or programmes a financial advantage. The FEFC also required that Colleges held a very sophisticated level of information on students and programmes.

In April 1993 the provision of Adult Education was transferred from LEA control to become part of the College. The result of this new responsibility was that the College now managed an extensive provision of courses delivered at community venues throughout the Huddersfield area. These courses ranged from academic programmes like GCSEs and A Levels to recreational courses like arts and crafts or sport.

In 1997 Dr Rossiter retired and the new Principal was appointed. Ms Jeanne Coburn took over responsibility for the College in a period when considerable demands were being made on the sector. Financial constraints forced the College to restructure its staff at the same time as meeting increasing recruitment, retention and quality standards. The other key priority to face the FE sector is the responsibility to encourage the participation in further education by individuals and groups who have not previously benefited from the experience. The Widening Participation agenda forms part of

the government's social inclusiveness policies and is designed to raise general standards of education throughout the UK. Despite these challenges, the College continues to grow and improve the quality of service it gives to its students, partners and clients.

Today, Huddersfield Technical College is one of the largest colleges in the region, attracting students locally, nationally and internationally to Huddersfield.

The College now operates regularly from over 40 different sites in addition to the main campus on New North Road, mainly in the Huddersfield area but also in North Kirklees and in the rural villages surrounding Huddersfield. In addition to centres offering a mix of vocational, non-vocational and basic education programmes the College runs specially developed courses in a further wide range of community centres and schools.

With 1,200 staff and over 23,000 students the College is a large community in its own right and its staff and students live in, work in and contribute to all the local communities that surround the College. One in four households in Huddersfield has a student at Huddersfield Technical College.

With huge investment in the College's new Engineering Technology Innovation Centre and the redevelopment of the historic Highfields site, as well as the commitment to delivering courses through new technologies, Huddersfield Technical College will continue to develop and extend the range of learning and training it offers to the people of Huddersfield, in the new millennium.

Top left: *Dr H T Taylor presenting awards to international students during the 1970s.* **Top right:** *Early computer classes.*
Left: *The premises today.*

What's new about learning?

Huddersfield New College was established with the amalgamation of Hillhouse Technical School and Huddersfield College at the beginning the school year 1957-58, though for two terms the combined schools continued to occupy their old buildings at Hillhouse and New North Road. Building work on the new school for 900 boys at Salendine Nook had commenced in August 1956 and the completed school was officially opened on 26 March 1958 by Sir Edward Boyle, Parliamentary Secretary to the Minister of Education. Pupils and staff moved into the new building at the beginning of the following summer term.

Huddersfield College, originally a public school, had been founded in 1838 to provide a grammar school education 'combined with moral and religious instruction' at an annual fee of eight guineas per pupil. The school closed as a public school in 1893 but was reopened as the College Higher Grade School by the Huddersfield School Board the following year, for both girls and boys. Following a report in 1904 the Board decided to establish a secondary school for girls at Greenhead, to convert Huddersfield College to a similar facility for boys and to build a new school at Hillhouse. Huddersfield College again became a boys' school in 1909. The new Hillhouse Central School took both girls and boys until 1923 when the Hillhouse School became boys only after a Central School for girls was established at Longley Hall.

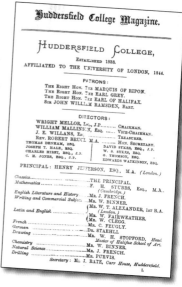

Both the Central School for girls at Longley Hall and the Hillhouse school developed strongly following the education act of 1944, both being designated Technical schools.

Above left: *HE Atkins, Principal in the early 1900s.*
Above right: *A school magazine dating from July 1877.* ***Below:*** *Huddersfield College First Team - 1914/1915.*

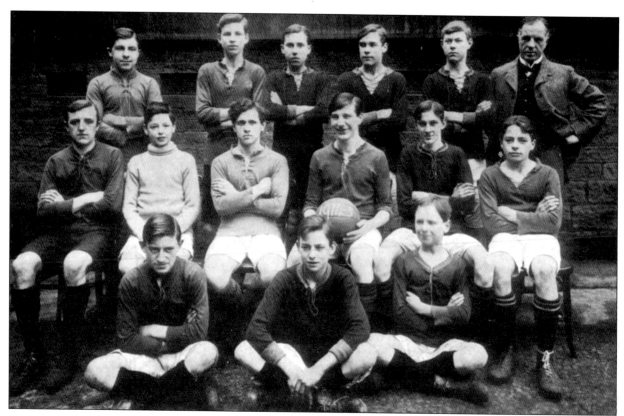

More architectural changes naturally followed: July 1997 saw the opening of the college's new two million pound teaching block. The official opening was performed by the chief executive of the Further Education Funding Council Professor David Melville. The new building would mainly benefit IT, business, media and modern languages and support up to 250 computer work stations. The building also provided a Study Centre in which students could obtain individual help, especially in the key areas of English, maths and information technology.

Despite, or perhaps because of, the various Huddersfield schools successes more change was proposed leading eventually to the building of New College.

The 65 acre site, shared by Huddersfield High School for Girls - as the old Central School was now known - and the Salendine Nook mixed secondary school, only contained two joint facilities: a swimming pool and a running track, otherwise the three schools ran independently of one another.

The popularity of New College meant that the library and dining areas were too small, and the science block heavily over-used. The library was extended and a new dining room constructed. In the intervening years many other improvements and changes have subsequently been made to the original buildings.

Other less visible changes have occurred at New College too, not least the arrival of girls as well as boys; most significantly however major reorganisation in the educational world led to New College becoming a sixth form college rather than one catering for students across the entire age range for secondary education.

Above: *The College in the 1960s and (inset) today.*
Top: *Teachers and staff in September 1971.*

Today Huddersfield New College is well established with 1,400 students and a good and consistent reputation for academic success and sporting excellence; music and performance arts are also highly regarded. Most students study for 'A' level examinations and there is a range of general vocational qualifications; each year the majority of students go on to university whilst those who choose to go into employment find that the qualifications they gained at the college gives them a head start in the jobs market.

The first headmaster was described by the School Inspectors in 1964 as having been appointed to Huddersfield College in 1948 after experience at four other grammar schools. According to the inspectors the school was fortunate to have such headmaster.

The most recent inspection in 1999 graded the College's performance as overwhelmingly outstanding or good, with no aspect of the college provision being judged less than satisfactory: today the headmaster may have been replaced by a female Principal but her zeal for excellence in education is every bit a match for her predecessors who have been educating us since the reign of Queen Victoria.

Counting on additions

Fred Sheard, who founded the firm of accountants which still bears his name was born at Thorpe, Almondbury on 19 October, 1872.

Having an aptitude for figures he joined the Huddersfield firm Poppleton, Appleby and Ward, accountants where he received a sound grounding in accountancy principles.

Shortly after his thirtieth birthday he set up his own business as a Certified Accountant. He worked from offices in 5 and 6 Kirkgate Buildings, Huddersfield which was the base for the firm for many years.

This was a propitious time to go into business as shortly after his departure from Poppleton, Appleby and Ward, Mr Ward left the firm; Poppleton and Appleby continued in partnership but moved out of Huddersfield. This left a gap in the provision of accounting services which no doubt Fred was happy to fill.

Over the course of time he was joined by his two sons Ernest and Percy, who were trained by their father and the firm changed its name to Fred Sheard & Sons. There must have been sufficient business to provide a comfortable living for all three as we hear of Fred standing as candidate in the 1911 Municipal Elections in the Moldgreen Ward. Listed among the reasons he gives for folk to give him their vote is 'Being in business on my own account, my time is absolutely

REASONS

WHY YOU SHOULD SUPPORT

MR. SHEARD.

1.—Because he is a Moldgreen Man, and knows the needs and requirements of the Ward.

2.—Because his time is at his own disposal, and he is willing to devote it to the service of his fellow Ratepayers.

3.—Because he will support the common sense management of the town's affairs.

4.—Because he is not bound by any Society or clique, and will watch over your interests without fear or favour.

5.—Because he does not make promises he cannot fulfil, but is prepared to support any practical proposals for the benefit of all sections of the ratepayers.

Above left: Fred Sheard, founder of the firm.
Above right: Fred Sheard's statement of promise from when he stood for council in the 1911 local elections. Below: Greenhead Park. Civic dignitaries and councillors (including Fred) waiting to greet King George V and Queen Mary in 1911 or 1912.

at my own disposal' and he was willing to devote it to the service of his fellow ratepayers.

His business life brought him into contact with many who had an interest in keeping the Rates down and a particular issue he wanted to raise on the Council was that a recent amalgamation of the Wards of the Borough and the consequent unification of the Rates had resulted in an extra 6d in the £ for the home-owners of Moldgreen. Fred Sheard did not consider that this increase had yielded any particular benefit to the residents but the restructuring had deprived the elected representatives of Moldgreen direct control of the highways passing through their area.

Financial responsibility was clearly of great interest to him as before he was twenty years old he was a member of a Friendly Society and served for many years as an office-holder. He was also concerned about efficiency and the common-sense and practical dischargng of official policy - he was an early enemy of red tape and bureaucratic extravagance. He had a principle of not making promises which he could not fulfill which is a quality many might wish was possessed by contemporary politicians.

Fred Sheard died at the age of 58 in March 1931 and Ernest and Percy continued in the family firm. In the 1950s they were joined by Frederick Sheard, son of Ernest Sheard, and Michael Dyson, at which time the firm became Chartered Accountants. At various stages the firm expanded its client base by purchasing blocks of audits in 1937 from EB Shaw and from George F Lee in 1969, who had practiced in the town as an unqualified accountant for many years. He joined Sheards as an employee for a time.

The 1970s was a time of great change in the firm. In the early part of the decade Richard A Sheard, son of Percy Sheard, and Brian Butterworth were both added to the list of partners having received their training and qualified while in the firm. Then in 1973 Percy Sheard died, leaving the firm in the hands of the third generation of Sheards and other partners, Ernest Sheard had retired some years earlier.

A dinner dance was held at Greenhead Masonic Hall to celebrate 75 years of the firm in 1978. It was attended by 110 present and former members of staff and guests including representatives of Henry Brook & Co Ltd who had been among Fred Sheard's original clients.

The firm acquired the business of JR Davison & Co to provide continuity for their clients around the time of the retirement of the Davison partners in 1984.

A major change occured in 1987 when the firm moved out of Kirkgate Buildings where it had started out. These premises were felt to be no longer suitable for modern professional offices and the firm is now located at Vernon House, New North Road, Huddersfield. The firm is currently run by Richard Sheard, grandson of the founder, Carolyn Atkinson and Kevin Winterburn; the other partners having retired.

Above centre: *An early letterhead.*
Left and below: *Today's partners (left) outside the New North Road premises.*

Sam Weller - a Dicken's of a story

The firm of Sam Weller & Sons, based at Holmfirth's Pickwick Mills, may have a Dickensian name but it is equipped with twenty first century technology.

The company was founded in 1911 by Sam Weller, a textile salesman with an office in Bradford's Swan Arcade from where he bought and sold cloth.

The firm moved three times in its first fifteen years, first to Richard Street then to Harris Street before moving to Peckover Street in Bradford's Little Germany.

Sam Weller junior was born in 1914, the youngest of four children. Sam junior joined the firm from school but sadly there was very little work to support him and so he left to work as a shipping clerk. His brother however stayed with Wellers through the war of 1939-45.

On the outbreak of the second world war, Sam Weller junior, despite poor health, was one of the first to join up and saw service in the UK.

In 1940 Sam married Freda Pickersgill, a local Bradford girl. On the cessation of hostilities and being demobbed young Sam returned to the family business.

Sam Weller junior managed the operation almost alone after the war and by the early 1950s the company was employing around 30 people.

Above left: *Sam Weller junior.*
Above right: *Sam Weller discussing production in the 1950s.* ***Below:*** *A van from the 1950s.*

South America. Elsewhere Sam Weller junior set up a link with a merchant in Germany who took care of European markets.

Wellers soon decided to manufacture its own cotton fabric and set up a weaving plant specialising in a product which they had previously only merchanted - 'decatising' wrappers sold to dyers and finishers for use in woollen and worsted fabric finishing; a product and process which would form the basis of the company's future.

The necessary looms were only obtained in 1952 because of the long wait for equipment after the war. This coincided with the opening of a weaving shed in Liverpool, then the centre of the cotton trade. Wellers began almost exclusively producing decatising wrappers: the looms having to be specially adapted to produce this special fabric. The weaving shed was purpose built. Weaving moved to the current premises in Holmfirth in 1957/58.

Business continued to grow: export orders were received from America, Australia, New Zealand and

Sam Weller senior, the company's founder, died in 1961 in Bognor Regis; he had originally come from East Grinstead and returned to the South on his retirement. Today Sam Weller junior's sons Tony and Chris run the company.

It wasn't really new to them however: both brothers had learned all aspects of the job, from the most menial to quality weaving, whilst working weekends and holidays. They both had a grounding in sales, when their father took them out on the road with him.

Operating on two sites: Holmfirth and Peckover Street, Bradford eventually became impractical. Warehousing and cloth-examining soon moved to Pickwick Mill and in 1991 the whole company moved to Holmfirth.

Today the company is famous for its fabrics, and also for its calendars, once hand-painted, with illustrations of Pickwickian scenes drawn by FG Lewin; like Wellers cloths these too are known world-wide.

Above centre: *A recent calendar.*
Top left: *Production methods in the 1950s...*
Top right: *...and today.*

Concocting the potent potion for enduring success

A Chemist's which has been a vital part of the local community in Golcar is approaching its first centenary of business and service.

Sam Thorpe Shaw who was born in Ossett but had begun a lifetime's association with the village when he came to live with his aunt, Mrs Thorpe in Golcar when he was seventeen. At that time he was apprenticed to his uncle, Mr Briggs the chemist, in Horbury. He served a two year articled apprenticeship and studied for a year at college to qualify as a Chemist and Druggist. It was in 1902, however, that he went into business on his own and starting in a small way gradually over the years built up a business which had branches all over the Huddersfield area.

The first shop was in James Street which he bought from Alderman S Stephens of Milnsbridge. His first week's takings amounted to £21. 9s 11d.

Village life without a chemist's shop is unimaginable as there are so many occasions when we need to buy treatment to relieve those irritating little complaints we all have from time to time; in addition in those days before the National Health Service, the chemist's role in the community was of greater significance than today as many folk could not afford the doctor's fees and the chemist was a valued source of help and advice for many. Chemists were often responsible for making up their own preparations and Sam was no exception, it must be impossible to estimate the number of folk in

Above: *Company founder Sam Thorpe Shaw.*
Right (both pictures): *The Thorpe family pictured in their home in the 1920s.*

and far beyond the Huddersfield area who have benefited from his Covonia and Elderflower Balm.

Three turnover figures tell their own story about the prosperity of the business and how the general affluence of a community affects those who rely on the purchasing power of those around it. In the 1922/23 period the turnover was £837, in 1926/27 it was £1121, however by 1932 the upward trend had been halted and the figure was down to £887, a reflection of the economic depression experience by many countries across the world at that time.

But the general trend was upward and the business thrived in James Street. In time there was quite a chain of chemist's shops throughout the area, including two in Golcar and others in Fartown, Bradford Road, Sheepridge, Rastrick, Elland, Stainland, Marsden and Uppermill; at the height of ST Shaw's business expansion programme there were no less than thirteen shops in all. This was the time when going to a shop was a completely different experience from what it is today; instead of picking up a basket and walking round a large store, you went up to the counter, often having caught up on the local news and gossip in the queue, and waited while the chemist weighed out the amount of Bicarb or Epsom Salts you wanted from his supply, putting it in handy brown paper bags with the company's own label on.

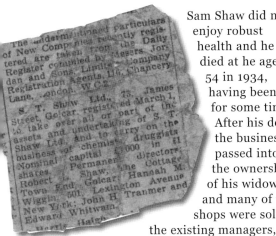

Sam Shaw did not enjoy robust health and he died at he age of 54 in 1934, having been ill for some time. After his death the business passed into the ownership of his widow, and many of the shops were sold to the existing managers, who had in fact all been his apprentices. It was Sam's practice to install as manager in a new shop men who had proved their competence and reliability as apprentices.

Special mention needs to be made of one such apprentice, Edward Whitwam who gave fifty years service to S T Shaw's, he was there for such a long time that there were many in the village who actually thought he was Mr Shaw! He was a well-liked and respected member of the local community and during his working life became an essential part of Golcar life. He had been born in Golcar in 1907 and he lived all his life there, choosing to

remain in that community in retirement. He loved his job and enjoyed serving the people of Golcar in his professional capacity, recommending medicines, dispensing them and even delivering them to homes not just in Golcar but scattered throughout the surrounding Pennine countryside. At the end of his working life he was serving the grandchildren of some he provided with medicines at the start of his career.

The ownership of S T Shaw's business passed jointly to his son R ('Bobby') L Shaw and his daughter Hannah Nixon on the death of their mother. Hannah was living with her husband in Liverpool and Bobby also had the responsibility for his own photographic processing business, R L Shaw Photographic, with branches throughout the North, so John Tramner was appointed as General Manager to run both the pharmacy and photographic sides of things on a day-to-day basis.

Above: The newspaper cutting announcing the takeover of the business by Robert Shaw and his sister Peggy Nixon following the death of their mother. **Below and right:** *A postcard produced by the firm of Apperley Bridge.*

At this time, the mid 1930s the threat of war was looming in the distance but pharmacists were exempt from the call-up and John was able to remain in his post throughout the war period.

Bobby retired in the 1970s and Peegy, now Mrs Wiggin, took over complete responsibility for the firm, a state of affairs which lasted for about the next twenty years. From that time the family business has been in the hands of the third generation of Shaws when Bobby's son Sam J Shaw took over the reins of the chemist shops, which still trade under the original name of S T Shaw.

Mr Harrison joined the company in the 1970s at about the time of the introduction of decimal currency. He recalls that the change brought benefits to the firm in ease of accountancy practices but that it received a rather less than enthusiastic reception from the customers.

A 'Sale of Poisons Register' in still in the company archives, covering the period 1936 to 1966, and this records that in 1948 no less than five sales of hydro-cyanic acid (cyanide to you and me) were transacted for the purpose of 'destroying dog' - these were hard days for the canine population of Golcar!

Today there are chemist shops trading in the Shaw name in Golcar, Fartown and Lindley. As is the case everywhere and for everything nowadays, the running of the company is chiefly carried out through computerised records. When the first system was introduced in 1985, it was a simple device for the printing of labels but now is considerably more sophisticated and encompasses stock levels of medications, patient records and ordering, and while the shops are still serving the people in those communities, the premises would be practically unrecognisable by the founder.

Above: *Bobby Shaw and friends.*
Below: *S T Shaw's premises in Golcar.*

Peering round the filing cabinet, it is difficult to be sure exactly what piece of office equipment is creating such interest. It looks rather like a new telex machine. The teleprinters attached to the old telex systems were huge machines, partitioned off from the rest of the office because they made such a racket, and the telex operator - often the only man in an office full of females - sat at the printer, in his or her own little booth. Later, telex machines became more sophisticated; whisper-quiet, they sat on a table in the corner of the office. These 1960s visitors to the Hanson Haulage Open Day, held to mark the opening of the new depot on Leeds Road, seem fairly intrigued - as no doubt today's younger generation would be,

though for different reasons. Technology in the office moved ahead in leaps and bounds during the second half of the 20th century. When fax machines came in during the 1980s, the concept of instantaneously transmitting a document to almost anywhere in the world seemed like something off Star Trek - beam it up, Scotty! And as for e-mail ... Modern telex machines represented one small step along the way, and in their day were considered state-of-the-art. But one disadvantage, from the operator's point of view, was that there was no means of erasing typing mistakes. So if you were having one of those days when there is a loose connection between your brain and your fingers, the file copies of telexes that you had sent could make you cringe with shame.

WT Johnson - a continuing story of finishing

A Huddersfield company producing world-class finishes for woollen and worsted cloth was founded in 1916 when Walter Thomas Johnson set up in business in premises on Wakefield Road. He had decided to take the brave step of branching out with his own company, aged about 50 years, after serving as Forman Finisher at Glendinning's. He took his son, Walter Marshall Johnson ('WM'), into partnership with him; this was a complete change of direction for the young Walter who had only recently passed his Civil Service exams.Today Walter Thomas's great-grandsons are continuing the family tradition, the fourth generation to be involved in the business.

For the first few years the two Walters, father and son, worked together but later Walter senior's other sons, Tom and Frank joined them, and the tradition that all family members would be fully acquainted with each and every part of the business began. Although over the years some Johnsons have inevitably spent more time on one area than another, they are all conversant with the technical side of things and endeavour to keep abreast of what is happening in the workshop and with their customers.

Below: *Early quality procedures, which would include burling and mending, the art of finding slubs in material and removing them.*

complexity to the procedure, the original raison-d'etre of the company remains the same as it was during World War I, namely to take woollen cloth as it comes straight from the loom and wash it (usually with soap and water), dry it and press it using the most up-to-date machinery. A great number of variations are now possible in each of these three stages of the finishing process, washing, drying and pressing thanks to the sensitvity of the modern computer-controlled machines. Today's customers demand repeatable finishes due to the popularity of 'mix and match' clothing - items of an outfit bought separately need to look good together, so the quality and uniformity of the finish is of paramount importance.

All companies need to stay ahead to stay in business and this is particlarly the case when the industry concerned is in decline as is the case with the woollen industry. Many mills in the West Riding which used to resound to the roar of busy weaving looms are now derelict and it is a testament to the

One of the first hurdles to be surmounted by the infant Johnson firm was to repay a personal loan granted by Mr Sykes of Norwood Green. He is also believed to have owned the premises occupied by the firm.Today the firm is still operating from the same address in Wakefield Road, Huddersfield but the site has seen significant expansion and development over the years. Much of this development took place in the 1950s when land adjacent to their site which had previously been Huddersfield Corporation allotments was acquired for new building work - indeed they would have liked more but this was not permitted.

In its infancy, the Colne Valley woollen industry was carried out by firms who did everything starting with the raw wool from the sheep, through spinning,weaving, dyeing and finishing. As time went on, however, some firms started to specialise on one process, Johnsons was obviously one of them, (though in the 1970s Johnsons took over Tom Lees & Co, Dyers from Honley, renaming the company DP Dyers Ltd). Concentrating on a specific area gave a number of advantages - they were able to build up expertise in that particular process and were able to direct their resources into the best available machinery for the job. Some like Crowther's continued to offer the entire range, but they were in the minority.

Though the equipment available for carrying out the finishing process has changed over time as technology has brought new levels of accuracy and

Above (both pictures): *Machines that would have been used by the company in the early days.*
Right: *An elevated view of today's premises.*

quality of the Johnson treatments that the company is still in business in this highly competitive international market for it is not only local firms which represent rival bidders for available work but also Italian companies which specialise in the same field as well as developing countries which have significantly lower labour costs.

The company employs over 90 people today and takes pride in providing a product which they believe is the best in the business, a result of the best eqipment available and nearly a century of Johnson expertise.

A key component in the success of the company has been its access to soft West Yorkshire water, one reason why at one time the woollen industry was able to thrive in the area. WT Johnson thought it would be a great advantage to the firm to have its own water supply on site brought directly from a well for two reasons: firstly they would not have to pay the water company to supply it, therefore minimising costs and, secondly, the water would be pure and not contain any additives making it ideal for washing the fabric. The Manchester firm of drilling experts, Thomas Matthews was consulted and having studied geological maps of the area felt sure that water would be found on the site and agreed to find it. Boring commenced in the late 1930s and the hole reached the depth of about 300 feet which was the standard well depth, but there was no water. Undaunted, Matthews kept drilling (and invoicing Johnsons accordingly). When the hole had reached a depth of 1000 feet, 'W T' felt that further expenditure could not be justified on what seemed to be a fruitless project and

called the drilling off. However Rex Matthews, who was supervising the operation, was so unshakeably convinced that water would be found that he said he would go on drilling and allow 'W T' to pay him back when he could - thus the Johnson firm received another huge benefit from a patient benefactor. Rex's confidence was not misplaced and water was indeed struck - at a depth of more than 1,500 feet (it is believed to be the deepest well in Yorkshire). The associated pipework was laid in 1940 and from that time the firm has reaped the benefit of its own uncontaminated free water-supply.

It is a point of pride in the company that they are suppliers of a process which meets important'-green' criteria: no detergents or synthetic additives are used in the processes and this gives the company a leading edge in today's marketing climate where 'natural' and 'sustainable' are coveted buzzwords. WT Johnson & Sons remain confident in their ability to stay ahead of the field in the future.

Above left: *The Johnson family today.*
Below (both pictures): *Today's Mold Green premises.*

The Holme of hot air

The company, which is now part of the giant American conglomerate Halliburton, has been an important contributor to the wealth of the Huddersfield area since 1850 when the WC Holmes & Company Ltd was established at the Turnbridge Works.

William Cartwright Holmes initiated design and production of plant for the treatment of gas installations and the recovery and refining of by-products. His innovations included a 'brush' washer which had a dramatic beneficial effect on the purification of coal-generated gas, and the company built up an impressive range of gas treatment products, including a revolutionary patented 'dri-gas' plant. This process involved the extraction of water vapor and naphthalene from the gas before it was sent into the distribution network and was adopted by many gas authorities, who were impressed by the smoother running of their services made possible by the improved quality of the gas going through the pipes. One gas company reported a drop in complaints from 200 to two per day and noticed considerable benefits as far the cost of routine maintenance was concerned.

Around the same time as the Holmes operation was getting off the ground in Huddersfield in the 1850s, two brothers, Philander and Francis Roots were developing a rotary positive air blower, known as the 'Roots Blower' in

Connersville, Indiana, USA. In 1927 WC Holmes built these blowers under a licensing agreement and continued to manufacture their own when the agreement expired, gradually improving the design.

The company traded as Peabody Holmes from 1973 until 1990 when it was taken over by Dresser Industries and became part of their Roots division. The Huddersfield works became the metric plant of the organisation and continues to be a leading force in the world-wide blower market.

In 1998, Dresser Industries merged with the Halliburton company to form the largest provider of products and services to the global petroleum and energy market. At the Huddersfield site, the company, which is now known as DMD-Roots, designs, manufactures and sells a range of air and gas blowers and vacuum pumps. The main markets served are water and wastewater treatment, bulk handling, process, chemical and petro-chemical, pulp and paper as well as general industry.

Top left: *Philander and Francis Roots.*
Above centre: *Early advertising.* **Right:** *Part of the Huddersfield facility.*

Summary justice is dished out to a pickpocket at a 1950s 'Town' match

Acknowledgments

Morris Bray, photographer of New North Road, Huddersfield
Geoff Lumb
Ian Thomas

The publishers would also like to thank Shirley Bostock, Brian Kilner and the many other friends and colleagues who helped in the preparation of the captions by sharing their knowledge and their own recollections.

Thanks are also due to
Margaret Wakefield who penned the editorial text and
Steve Ainsworth for his copywriting skills